TALKING T

Acknowledgements

American publishers have collected together anthologies of work from the American gay press – notably *Christopher Street* and *Gay Sunshine*; no such attempts have been made in this country and, thus, countless millions of words about our own experiences have probably been lost for ever. The interviews in this book have been selected from work published between 1970 and 1991. One of my reasons for wishing to preserve them is because I suspect they contain information which may be of use to future generations of biographers, critics or social historians.

The interview with Colin Spencer appeared in *Transatlantic Review*; an extended version of the interview with Robin Maugham appeared in *Gay Sunshine*; those with Quentin Crisp, Christopher Isherwood, Francis King, Gavin Lambert, John Lehmann and Michael Wilcox in *Gay News*; that with Edmund White in *Him* (which subsequently became *Gay Times*); those with Neil Bartlett, Steven Corbin, Patrick Gale, Damon Galgut, Stephen Gray, Joseph Hansen, Patricia Highsmith, Alan Hollinghurst, Timothy Ireland, Larry Kramer, Hanif Kureishi, Brian Masters, David Rees, Peter Robins, Martin Sherman and Kenneth Williams in *Gay Times*.

Thanks are due to Denis Lemon (John Lehmann), Michael Mason (Francis King and Christopher Isherwood) and Richard Smith (Neil Bartlett) for permission to reproduce interviews co-written with them; to Hugh Miller who operated the cassette-recorder at several of the interviews; and Sebastian Beaumont who typed the manuscript.

Peter Burton, Brighton, 1991

Talking to . . .

Peter Burton
in conversation with

Neil Bartlett
Steven Corbin
Quentin Crisp
Patrick Gale
Damon Galgut
Stephen Gray
Joseph Hansen
Patricia Highsmith
Alan Hollinghurst
Timothy Ireland
Christopher Isherwood
Francis King
Larry Kramer
Hanif Kureishi
Gavin Lambert
John Lehmann
Brian Masters
Robin Maugham
David Rees
Peter Robins
Martin Sherman
Colin Spencer
Edmund White
Michael Wilcox
Kenneth Williams

Writers writing on gay themes

THIRD HOUSE (PUBLISHERS)

First published 1991 by Third House (Publishers)
69 Regent Street, Exeter EX2 9EG, England

World Copyright © Peter Burton 1991

ISBN 1 870188 17 9

Typeset by Bookman Ltd, Bristol BS3 1DX

Printed by Billing & Sons, Ltd., Worcester

Distributed in the United Kingdom and in Western Europe
by Turnaround Distribution Co-op Ltd., 27 Horsell Road,
London N5 1XL

Distributed in the United States of America by InBook,
140 Commerce Street, East Haven, Connecticut, 06512,
U.S.A.

Distributed in Australia and New Zealand by
Stilone Pty. Ltd., P.O. Box 155, Broadway,
New South Wales 2007, Australia

Cover Photograph: Bill Short

Contents

For

Michael Lowrie

and

Richard Smith

with love

and

for

Maud and Ben

who are always there

Neil Bartlett

At the age of thirty-two, Neil Bartlett has perhaps already proved himself the most creatively adventurous gay man in Britain.

Even before *A Vision of Love Revealed in Sleep* – his meditation on the life of the Pre-Raphaelite artist Simeon Solomon – he had devised and appeared in a series of stimulating and controversial performance pieces. *Vision* was seen in three incarnations over four years, each more ambitious than the last and each garnering praise from the straight and gay press alike. His highly-acclaimed *Who Was That Man?* – an homage to Oscar Wilde – was one of the most important and readable pieces of gay historical contemplation to have appeared in this country.

In the past year his translation of Racine's *Bérénice* has been staged at the National Theatre; his adaptation of Molière's *School for Wives* was the final production under Anne Castledine at the Derby Playhouse; and his new stage work (with Nicholas Bloomfield) *Sarrasine* (from a story by Balzac) has already played at the Edinburgh Festival, is currently at London's Drill Hall Arts Centre, and will tour until Christmas.

Bartlett's first novel *Ready to Catch Him Should He Fall* has just been published and it is no exaggeration to say that it stands head and shoulders above any British or American gay novel to have appeared in several years. *Ready to Catch Him Should He Fall* is (to use a journalistic cliché) a searingly honest evocation of gay life, cultures and rituals; it is tender, brutal, explicit, erotic and moving – set in a nameless but eternal city and with a time-scale that can only be defined as fluid. The novel centres on the relationships between Boy (a young man seeking experience), O (his older lover), and Mother (their protector); and their love and care for each other and of the other inhabitants of The Bar, the locus of their interactions. Above all, this enormously impressive and exciting novel – a fictional debut of staggering assurance and ability – reveals the depths of Bartlett's commitment to our history, our present and our future.

On a brilliantly sunny Sunday in Brighton we sat over a long lunch and discussed Bartlett's theatre work and – most of all – *Ready to Catch Him Should He Fall*.

You've had a busy year . . .

'It has been an incredible year and one thing that's really exciting about it is that it finally gets me out of the hole of "What do you do? Who are you?" With this year's work I can say, "Well, *you* tell *me* what I do. You take Racine, Molière, Balzac and the novel and *A Vision of Love Revealed in Sleep* and you tell me what I do. You tell me if I am a gay artist, or theatre artist, or performance artist, or novelist" – because I no longer have to talk about that . . . '

Although *Ready to Catch Him Should He Fall* is set in a city that is recognisably London, it is never identified as such – why was that?

'The novel was written in a lot of different places. Not deliberately. I didn't think "Oh, it would be good to include a variety of places in the book." Wherever I was, because of work or for other reasons, I would write, and when I'd done it I realised that what was important to me was that it wasn't a description of a particular place. It was to do with why the bar is called The Bar and is every bar I have ever been in. It's that sense of there are so many places and so many encounters in the kind of gay life that I lead – but one senses that lurking beneath them is the archetype, socially and sexually, *especially* sexually, and romantically. There's the original. The one. And that's why the bar is called The Bar and that's why Boy is called Boy and that's why O is called O; and, again, I didn't let it happen deliberately. I just let it . . .

'I didn't want the book to be seen as about "gay life in London," because if you say that it's immediately perceived by someone who's picking up the book as being a realistic account of a realistic situation. Which it isn't. And so although the city is London, it's not . . . the city is London in the same way as in *Who Was That Man?* It is London, but it continually changes its shape. You could turn a corner or open a door and suddenly you're in a city that you don't quite recognise.'

And the book is not set in any recognisable time . . .

'It clearly is set now, or the action of the story takes place now, except the people keep describing it as "Well, of course, in those days, when this happened, life was like this." But there are very strong elements of previous periods of gay life. I mean, it goes into – not exactly time-slips – but without being able to say exactly where and when it happens you are in a different era of the city's life. Going back to the nineteenth century, but also the nineteen forties, fifties, sixties, seventies.

'The book is a return to a lot of very deeply held beliefs. Things very deep inside me which are to do with my life and my parents and the way I was brought up, and my family, and that's why the book is dedicated to my two grandmothers. Out of respect for them and the part that the world they represent has played in my life.'

The book does seem to have a certain religious feel to it . . .

'It's not intentional. It's probably a reflection of how deeply it is in me. Intellectually it wasn't planned and I surprised myself with that aspect of it. I think in a sense that some ritual is being enacted, and clearly the ritual is the standard narrative of love: love, courtship, marriage, child. (I did have *The Book of Common Prayer* open on my desk the whole time I was writing the novel.) I'm not religious now and I don't go to church, but, like anyone who is brought up with it, I know my way around *The Book of Common Prayer* and the idea that the book can have services and ceremonies in it for every occasion of your life. Of course, the fact of the matter is that as a gay man I don't suppose that *The Book of Common Prayer* in a literal or obvious way has a ceremony in it for any occasion. That's exactly the contradiction that the novel is about – so having no ceremonies of our own, we invent new ones.'

The sex in *Ready to Catch Him* seems to be or to become sacramental . . .

'Of course! Sex is! But what happens is like we say we are inventing new sounds but of course you can't. There are shapes of desire and of love – because love has a shape – they aren't abstract energy. The shape of love must be informed, either positively or negatively, by the traditions that are inside you, whether you like them or not.

'Now I'm not being fatalistic about it and saying therefore that we are inescapably conditioned to see ourselves as surrogate heterosexuals doomed to re-enact the rituals of that conditioning. And that process operates both positively and negatively throughout the book – it glorifies the images; it makes glorious the loves that are being described.

'I have an image of the artist as being someone who is conductor of or receptor for my culture – and things are going through me which are larger than myself. I am using the language; I am talking about incidents and images which don't belong to me. On a literal level there is so much in that book which is inspired by the quality of other parts of the history of gay writing. But also in a larger sense, like with the character of Mother; already four people have told me that they know who she is. They've said, "Oh, it's great that you've put her in the book, but you're too young, how did you possibly know about her?" And then they tell me about either a woman or a drag queen they knew who was exactly like her. So clearly in creating that figure – for instance – and in Boy and O as well – I'm using images of people that don't just belong to me but are part of gay culture or the scene.'

What you have done in *Ready to Catch Him* – and what you did in *Who Was That Man?* – was put that history and that sense of continuity together in a form that is assimilable by most people . . .

'Yes, but it has a very odd effect, that detail, because it must be read so completely differently by people who

4

don't know – and yet it has a very real effect for those people . . .

'One of the things I try and do when I'm writing is to be able to talk about a dress or a club and have some sense of tangibility. That it isn't just some vague throwback to those days. That it was real, and it's as real as your memories as a homosexual. So I do that terrible thing of phoning people up at eleven o'clock at night and saying, "What make-up would she have worn in 1954?" and "Does pan-stick have a hyphen?" Because if one of those things is wrong then I feel I let people down. It's so disrespectful to talk about these things and get them wrong.'

Clearly you believe that gay life has a sound-track.

'Yes. One of my favourite moments in my translation of *The Misanthrope* is this very grand speech where Alceste talks about being driven insane by love but no one else understands. I'd translated it very faithfully. I didn't cheat. It just so happens that you can translate it as "and does no one know it's like I'm losing my mind." And you could always tell if there were queens in the audience because there'd be a little shriek at that point, that there should be Sondheim there. I think there's this marvellous moment when the heights of emotion which we normally think of as being described as High Art are described in exactly the same language as musicals or pop songs. And that's why all the great love scenes in the novel can be done to Mozart or to the lyrics of *Do you really want to hurt me?*'

It's very strange in gay fiction to find someone so affectionate about the gay scene . . .

'Well, it's a fantasy that I have. But in the same way that the book is a sequence of fantasy events. It's wishful thinking on my part, the idea that the bar could somehow be a place where there are relationships as deep as the relationships in the book. But of course I think it happens; I have been in places and seen men looking after each other – and that's what we're talking about.

'In 1985 I was in Toronto and I was hanging out with a bunch of four men who shared a flat and were known as The Family (and their names actually appear in the book.) There was this great weekend when one of The Family had split up with his boyfriend and the other two decided this was a mistake and that they should get back together again. They spent the whole weekend on the phone and in the bars, bringing these two guys back together again. And at the end of the weekend there was this fabulous tear-stained scene on the Sunday night and they kissed in the bar. One of them was the barman and the other guy jumped across the bar and kissed him – and everyone in the bar applauded. Everyone knew what was going on. And I was very young and very stoned and very in awe of these terrific men. I just thought that was the most marvellous thing. That a man should do that.'

I've propounded in print several times that homosexual life is – certainly potentially – far richer and far more sustaining than heterosexual life because heterosexual life looks inward, whereas gay life can be far more outward-looking . . .

'I think it's very important to talk about how very many different ways of doing it there are, in the same way as there are very many different ways of doing heterosexual relationships. I don't think it breaks down as a dichotomy. But the vast majority of gay people are raised by families. That's what we know about. It's the beginning of our lives. So I think the hunger to claim that life-bond of deep relationships is profound. I think that's where all that energy in the book comes from – the desire for that.'

The narrator often appears as this whingeing character . . . Do you ever feel distanced as an artist, an observer, from other gay men?

'It's funny. I don't think the narrator is particularly distanced. Sure, of course I do feel distanced at times, but doesn't everyone? Everyone feels that he's looking at things from the outside. No. That's not true. I'm evading the question. Yes. I sometimes feel that I am so aware of the complications of any given situation that I'm incapable of being . . . I'm very conscious that if I'm in a bar I'm always reading everyone's stories. I'm obsessive when it comes to making things mean something. And so, often, I'll find myself in a place, watching and listening and thinking rather than . . . It's because of my job, as an

6

artist I don't have a sense of work and leisure time. The gay world, what you'd call the scene, is about leisure time. As an entertainer I make things that people consume in their leisure time – books and performances – so that gives me a very unusual relationship to that culture. If I'm in a pub I'm quite likely to be sitting there thinking, "I wonder what is the film or book that this lot could come and see." So immediately they're "them" – because I'm in a relationship to "them" in so far as I make things that they consume. I sell and they buy. I think that's a useful way of describing my position. An outsider.

'It's a bit of a problem when someone beautiful comes up to you and says "Hello" and you think "Oh!" and you look at him and he says, "I've just read your book." And you think, "Yes. Yes. Later. Let's talk about it *much* later – like over breakfast!" That's very odd. When you're writing a book there is something peculiarly frightening about putting what you really think about life down on paper. And when it's finished, people you don't know (and you don't even know they're doing it) can pick it up and open it and they think they know what you know about life.

'Being held responsible for one's work is sometimes very hard! And you mustn't think about that whilst you're making it, because if you do, *forget it*! Your hands freeze . . . '

Don't you think straight people are going to find the book rather baffling?

'Well, people say that but . . . Jeanette Winterson gets asked the same thing and says, "I've never had any trouble understanding *Wuthering Heights*." That's a good answer. Books are about other people's lives. I don't know. I think the book will be castigated for being baffling. They'll say "Who could possibly be interested in what a few men do in a bar late at night?" There's nothing you can do about that. It's certainly not a book written to please people. Sometimes you want to write something that's going to be totally impenetrable to anybody but your immediate peers.'

Couldn't that cause people to level at you the accusation that you suffer from a ghetto mentality?

'The idea of a ghetto mentality is a joke in this country
. . . If there were a ghetto here I'd go and live in it. You
know you get people saying: "Does being gay influence
your work?" I just look them in the face and say, "Oh,
no, not at all." It has become a redundant question to
me, finally, which is great because I've had enough of that
question. If someone can't see that I am as much a gay
artist when I am producing a play written three hundred
years ago about an eighteen-year-old girl as when I'm
doing a cock-sucking scene in the new book, then I give
up. My work is a sufficient answer to that question.'

Steven Corbin

Born and raised in Jersey City, New York, a graduate of the University of Southern California (where he studied film writing) and now resident in Los Angeles, thirty-five-year-old Steven Corbin is currently enjoying acclaim for his first published novel: *No Easy Place to Be*.

Following the lives of three black sisters – Miriam, Velma and Louise (the latter of whom can 'pass' for white) – the book is a leisurely attempt to rediscover and recreate that particularly creative period in the nineteen twenties – known as the Harlem Renaissance – when black American creativity burst into full flower and public prominence and was (albeit briefly) 'taken up' by both the literati and Manhattan society.

Recently in London – he'd like to make Europe ('Paris or London') his home base – Corbin proved to be an attractive and articulate man, coincidentally overjoyed to talk to the British gay press because our American counterparts had all but ignored the book. Corbin feels that black writers are still somewhat marginalised in America – 'We're only allowed one black ikon at a time and since his death two years ago no one has replaced James Baldwin' – and nowhere more so than in his native gay press.

We talked about the Harlem Renaissance – tossing out names of some of the more interesting people involved (Langston Hughes, inevitably, Nella Larsen – both back in print in this country from Serpent's Tail – and the white Carl van Vechten) before settling down to bottles of mineral water and serious questions.

What caused you to choose the Harlem Renaissance as the subject for your novel?

'I grew up with my maternal grandmother. In the tradition of a tribal griot, she would tell us stories about our ancestors and where we came from and also about the period when she was a young girl in Harlem,' Corbin began. 'Namely, she spoke reverently of the Harlem Renaissance of the nineteen twenties, the golden age of Harlem that was vibrant and glamorous when she was a young girl. My grandmother never called that period the Harlem Renaissance. She talked about how people dressed up with no particular place to go but to be seen parading on Seventh Avenue, about Lena Horne as a young girl at the Cotton Club . . .

'Years later, when I was a student, I studied the period. University gave me a bigger sense of what it was all about. Then, when I'd decided to become a novelist rather than a screenplay writer, a friend asked me if I'd ever consider writing a period piece. I said I'd maybe think about writing about the Harlem Renaissance – and began immediately what turned out to be two years of research.'

How is that period regarded today – by black America?

'The Harlem Renaissance is an obscure period, even in black America. But that was true at the time – the average Harlemites – if you stopped them on the street and asked them about it – wouldn't have known what it was. The Harlem Renaissance is this chapter in American cultural history that has been closed. I felt it had to be brought to light again. *No Easy Place to Be* was a wonderful opportunity to tell a story to engage the average reader. It was glamour – but it was also a real explosion of talent only sixty years after slavery. People don't know what the Harlem Renaissance was . . .

'Americans don't know about their writers. It's one of the things that I abhor. If asked, most Americans would tell you that Stephen King's the greatest American writer – not that I want to put him down. White Americans will only read black authors when an Alice Walker *The Colour Purple* comes along.

'And we're a very illiterate society. People are only interested in electronic forms of escapism – music, movies, television. Lazy forms of entertainment. Literature is so important to me and I would rather be in a space where it's appreciated . . . '

What made you choose three women as your central characters?

'Because there are more fictional possibilities with women,' Corbin answered. 'By writing about women, I could really make a point about the issue of race in America. For example, though the Cotton Club was in Harlem only white people were allowed in as customers. The women who worked at the club had to be black but they had to *look* white; the same wasn't true for the men who worked there – it didn't matter what colour the musicians were . . .

'There are also better possibilities with writing about women in that women tend to be more open among themselves than men – heterosexual men – who are much more guarded.

'Miriam, the eldest of the three sisters, is on a voyage of self-discovery – both by following Marcus Garvey and in sexual terms. I felt I could illustrate the point better with a woman – the dichotomy of dealing with oppression *and* blossoming sexuality. I used women as my main characters because I thought it was a lot more effective to show things from their perspective. Men are used as a backdrop . . . '

Why did you make Miriam a lesbian? Was it because so many of the recognised black women of that period – and later – have been acknowledged as lesbian or bisexual?

'No. I wanted gay characters in the book and I wanted to write about a gay character outside my own experience. Rudy – the gay man who is involved with Velma, the second sister – has some similarities to myself, though he isn't an extension of my own character. But the book has an eclectic cross-section of characters and I thought I'd like to explore and tell a gay woman's story. Sexuality and homosexuality were very much a part of the Harlem Renaissance. Rudy has gotten in touch with his sexuality; he knows who he is. I wanted to tell the story of someone who's making that discovery. Anyway, I already had two sisters who were heterosexual; I wanted some diversity.'

Did you find it difficult to get into the minds of your female characters?

'No. I've been asked if I "researched" women. I didn't. My family on my mother's side was female dominated, very matriarchal. When I was a kid growing up – listening to the stories my grandmother told – my mother and all her sisters and all their children spent time with my grandmother. In a sense I became a voyeur as a child – listening, observing. So when I sat down to do the book, it came very naturally. I've also been friends with a lot of women. But it was a challenge and I wasn't sure if I was capturing a woman's psyche. That's what propelled me: the challenge.'

And what made you choose to make one of your two main male protagonists – Rudy – gay, and the other – Scott – distinctly ambivalent?

'I wanted to say something about that particular scenario. Most gay men have had a Scott in their lives at some time.' Corbin grinned. 'Or maybe I've had Scotts for everyone. I have met men in my life who are sexually ambivalent. It's a very interesting perspective that I wanted to explore. People have asked me why the relationship between Rudy and Scott wasn't consummated, why they didn't do it – but that's because that's the course that that kind of relationship usually takes.

'Rudy was like writing myself into the Harlem Renaissance. Half the writers involved were gay – Langston Hughes, Counte Cullen, Claude McKay, Richard Bruce Nugent, for instance. Critics in the States have asked me why I've written about this aspect – but that's because they're so fucking homophobic. How could I *not* write about the gay men of that period?'

Did the white patrons – like Mrs Vanderpool in the novel – really have contracts with the artists they supported? Did they really control the creative output?

'Absolutely. It's another very true element in the novel. The patrons like Mrs Vanderpool were vastly manipulative, very into control and power. On the surface it looked like they were giving artists freedom but really they weren't. But those writers and artists weren't always

12

able to make a living – just like today. Sometimes I even wish I had a patron.

'It's true that a lot of writers of the period had patrons – after all, patrons knew everyone, they were well connected. Of course, there were writers who refused offers of help . . . '

Do you think that those white patrons – of whom Carl van Vechten must be counted one – were giving patronage or simply being patronising?

Corbin pondered the question for a moment. 'A little bit of both,' he said. 'Carl van Vechten had a very sincere approach to black artists. He was honourable in his intentions. In effect he was saying: "We have to pay attention to these people, we have to perpetuate this work." He was the exception to the rule. On the whole I think the patrons were patronising and condescending. *He* had a very genuine approach. There should be more van Vechtens . . . '

No Easy Place to Be is very open-ended. Are you planning a sequel?

'I'm not necessarily planning a sequel, no. I must move forward. I would have to feel that a sequel was "asking" to be done. With this one it was as if the characters were inside me waiting to get out. A sequel? I doubt it – but I never say "never" . . . '

And the future?

'I've got rewrites to do on my second novel, *Fragments That Remain* . . . which features an inter-racial male relationship. My publisher thinks it could be controversial.'

Quentin Crisp

The appearance is no longer startling: make-up on men has become a commonplace. The blue rinse seems almost conservative: in the past few years we have become accustomed to hair dyed all the colours of the rainbow. The voice is gentle and has about it more than a trace of mild bemusement. The fame which has come with old age came as a surprise: one suspects that if anonymity again descended it would not be unexpected. The wit and wisdom remain unchanged, with a distinct suggestion that here is a man who has not stopped thinking and who formulates his pearls with care and seriousness.

Quentin Crisp is home after almost a year in America; a year during which he became the kind of person others would risk their lives for as they darted through the Manhattan traffic to ask 'Didn't I see you on television?' He is back in England in the bedsitter in Chelsea in which the dust has accumulated for forty years. Squalor with style.

He is home for a brief visit – to promote his new book, *How to Become a Virgin*; his album *An Evening with Quentin Crisp*; and the return of his one-man show of the same name.

'Poor man's coffee' – or tea – is offered. We have brought Guinness with us – remembering from past meetings that Quentin is partial to a drop of the Irish elixir – and that's what we all settle for. Bob Workman crouches in a corner with his camera. I perch on a swivel chair and switch on my cassette-recorder, praying as I do so that our conversation will be heard above the roar of traffic along Beaufort Street.

14

'I'm only back probably until September,' Quentin announces. 'Because it's so hot in the summer in New York. People say to me, "Do you find it difficult to sleep in the night in New York?" That, of course, is the wrong question. It is impossible to stay awake during the day.'

We settle with our cans of Guinness; glasses are found.

'I did have a room in New York, on 14th Street. It was only twenty-six dollars a week – that's about twice as much as this room and half as big.'

'I am going to put the tape near you,' I say, moving the machine nearer the seat into which Quentin Crisp has settled.

'Right. And I will declaim.'

We start to talk about London.

'Yes, London is smaller, and I got told off for saying that the English have become an embittered race. But they have. I've been living in America as an ordinary mortal, because when I went in 1977 I went at the invitation of Mr Bennett and stayed at the Drake Hotel, and even when I went to work for Mr Elkins I went to live in the Algonquin, and when I went to Los Angeles I lived in the Beverly Wilshire Hotel – all this isn't the kind of life I know and understand. When I lived on 14th Street, I lived exactly as I live here. And it's freer, livelier . . . this dream that New York is grim and that people walk in great droves looking neither to right nor left, it's all untrue. New York is a leisurely city and people wander about. In summer there are men of my age with nothing on but their running shorts walking up and down 14th Street.

'There is nothing you can do on 14th Street which can cause you to be laughed to scorn because you're ugly, which is partly because it's America and partly because it's a part of a city which is cosmopolitan – on a lower scale, but which is nevertheless up to 30th Street; Spanish is spoken for a start . . . and therefore the pretty girls with the artificial flowers in their hair are part of American life. And I like very much when you travel by bus everybody speaks to everybody else. It's like being on a school outing. Someone says, "Where are you going?" and you say, "Perry Street," and someone says, "This bus doesn't go to

Perry Street," and someone else says, "Yes it does." "Yes it does," "No it doesn't" – and you involve everybody. And when you get off, everybody says, "Goodbye. Have a good day." And someone said to me, "Of course, it's all superficial." How can it be anything else? We're all total strangers. So, I love it. To me, any city is the people. So, if I went to Athens and said Athens was adorable, it wouldn't be because of the Acropolis, it would be because of the Greeks. But, in fact, I can't go anywhere where what I say is not understood. So I've been . . . I haven't been to South Africa . . . otherwise, I've done them all. It would be nice to go to South Africa and say, "What is Apartheid?" '

Have you been invited?

'I mentioned this at lunch, and Mr Goldman said, "There was a suggestion that you should go." But I've been to Australia and Canada and to America and Northern Ireland and Scotland and England; that's really all.'

American society doesn't seem to be based so much on envy.

'No. Exactly. It is an optimistic society. If you have any success, especially undeserved, in England, it provokes people. They say, "I could do that. My child, aged eleven, could do that." Whereas in America this inspires hope, and this makes a great difference. It's absolutely true. Anything you do in America inspires hope. Quite, quite wonderful.'

And once you're there, do you think you'll stay there for ever?

'I shall try and stay there permanently. I've had my confrontation with the immigration, and stamped in my passport are the mystic words, "Temporary evidence of permanent residence." And this, according to the lawyer, and I hope she's right, entitles me to whizz about the world without a visa and work without a permit. There are people who say I will never get any more – that I will go back every January and say, "What can you do for me?" and they will say, "Who are you?" rather than give me resident status, and I do see that this saves them the bother of answering either of the fatal questions. They don't have to answer the question, "How dare you let this terrible man into the United States?" because the answer is, "We are not letting him in." And they don't have to answer the question, "How *could* you be so heartless as to keep Mr Crisp out of the United States?" because the answer is, "But we haven't kept him out of the United States." And with this I must be content. But I must go as though I was going to live there for ever, because it would be a sin to keep a room on a reduced rent which I only use a few weeks a year. I've been away almost a year and it's not fair. So I will pack up everything. It's no good taking the furniture; it would fall apart before it was packed. But I will take all the clothes. Then I will go there and sleep on people's bathroom floors until I find a room.

'I would like a room a little bigger than the room I had for twenty-six dollars, so that I could burn some toast. But the milk wouldn't last the afternoon in the summer in Manhattan. *Here* the world is your refrigerator, but there you would need a tiny ice-box. You get your heat and light thrown in in rooming-houses, however low and degraded they may be. So really, the rent is hardly that much more. I hadn't thought about that before. Even the stairs and the halls and the loos are warm, whereas here one has to decide whether to go to the loo now or in the spring, it's so cold outside this room. I will go there and I'll brazen it out.'

Are you going to work there?

'I will work if work comes along. If I'm a resident alien, I'm free to work. I must never become an actor, but if I'm a pseudo-writer or a pseudo-lecturer I can get work. I'll never get regular work, my age is against that. So we'll take what money we can out of England and take it to America, and we might even get . . . I don't want to gamble, but I would like to know if there is any way I can get twelve per cent rather than two per cent. You need never buy food, the people are so hospitable.'

Are you planning to do any more writing?

'Well . . . I hope I've written the last book. I don't really like writing books. I know that one of the culture papers said I could go on writing my autobiography for ever, but when I was in New York I wrote tiny little pieces about classical movie stars, and though I only wrote six of them I could write sixty of them as well, and then maybe they could be collected together as a book. I'm not really a writer. The idea of going all the way to Timbuktu and writing about it – that's not for me.'

Does Quentin find that London has changed since he has been in America?

'Not at all. I notice the difference between the treatment I received in America when I first went and the gay papers were either indifferent or hostile, and now they are either indifferent or friendly.'

They treat you like an institution?

'Well, yes. One thing could have happened. They could have abandoned their hope. I think they thought, when I first arrived on MacDougal Street, that I was someone who had hired the theatre in order to deliver a manifesto and when they realised I was only a hired person I think their love for me died. Which is only understandable. Now they don't seem to do that. I don't ever read gay papers, unless someone shows them to me. That's because I don't read anything. Here they're still cross with me for the sake of it, which is understandable. I understand that.

'When I was in Cambridge for a signing session, they were picketing the shop; they were outside the shop saying what a mistake I was – but whether they are trying to change the bookshops or whether they are trying to change me, I don't know. But there's no doubt whatsoever, I am a heterosexual's idea of a homosexual. I am reassuring. And they know I am harmless.'

I ask Quentin about his feelings that *Gay News* had been hostile to him, an area for comment which is given a certain amount of space in *How to Become a Virgin*.

'I wouldn't have seen it; someone else pointed it out to me. Someone had written the *The Naked Civil Servant* should have been published posthumously. But Mr Lemon is politeness itself. He never puts a foot wrong.'

How does Quentin find American gays compared to their British counterparts?

'They do have humour . . . you see, it's different in New York. In Manhattan the prevailing passion for the "big time" is so great that you are almost instantly redeemed, and before you are redeemed they don't say, "What a fool he is for looking so odd;" they just wonder whether you'll actually make it to the big time – in which case they will dye their hair.'

And once he has sloughed off England, will Quentin miss his notorious bed-sitting room?

'I shall miss the room,' Quentin says. 'I wish I could take it with me. But I can't. So I shall have to be brave. Do you realise that I shall be a hundred and twelve before I have a room in New York that is as dusty as this one?'

Patrick Gale

Patrick Gale's first and second novels (*The Aerodynamics of Pork* and *Ease*) were published simultaneously in 1986, when he was twenty-four. He has subsequently published *Kansas in August* and *Facing the Tank* to critical acclaim: a reviewer in *The Listener* describing him as 'bound for greatness.' He is also a regular contributor to a range of publications, including *The Daily Telegraph* and *Gay Times*.

Gale's most recent novel, *Little Bits of Baby*, focuses on Robin, who – at the outset of the book – is about to be recalled to life after eight years of self-imposed retreat in an island religious community. Very much a tale of two cities – the London he left behind and the London to which he returns, *Little Bits of Baby* is a sometimes comic, sometimes touching and sometimes astringent look at attitudes and values in Thatcherite Britain.

How did he start writing?

'I can't honestly remember . . . it's always seemed such a natural activity. I was filling note-books with highly involved and, as often, not completed stories from an early age. I wrote a sheaf of truly awful plays in a creative writing class at Winchester and some lurid stories for various short-lived school magazines. Then writing took a back seat to acting for a while. I knew I could write, but acting was a challenge and I wanted to be Dirk Bogarde, an actor who wrote on the side. This was still my idea when I took my first job after Oxford. I was trying to get my Equity card by working as a singing waiter in an all-night restaurant. *The Aerodynamics of Pork* started life as a fistful of closely scribbled order pads, filled up during the nightly lull between midnight and four thirty.'

Do you utilize much personal experience in your novels?

'I think I'd be very foolish not to – either that or extremely gifted. Comedy (by which I mean writing that aims to induce some sort of "up" in the reader) must have its roots in the familiar and the true. However wild and wish-fulfilling their conclusions, each of my comedies takes root in an impulse I have felt for a situation I have been in. That said, I am not, nor have I ever been a lesbian policewoman . . . '

By contemporary standards, you are remarkably prolific – five novels since 1986 – is this because you find writing easy, that you feel you have a lot to say? Do you have plots and characters desperate to get out?

'I only *seem* prolific. There was some delay in publishing my first two novels and, since I write a novel a year, the backlog is only just easing up. Anyway – the first three are very short. (Why am I so defensive?) I write to live and until my publishers' advances swell to Jackie Collins proportions, I shall have to continue at a rate of one a year. I am slowing down, though. This is partly because I now have a dog and a lover (e.g. someone to talk to besides my typewriter), partly because I'm having to take on a lot more magazine and newspaper work to compensate for the Lawson effect, but mainly it's because I no longer feel I have to prove anything. I've carved myself a small niche and now I'm quietly expanding it. But, yes, in answer to your question, I do have a lot more to say (dog and lover notwithstanding) and I have to make a real effort not to start making mental sketches for a new novel when I've already got one in progress. Each novel tends to undergo violent developments between the first and second drafts because of homeless new plot ideas which force their way in.'

Your novels somehow seem all of a piece; one feels, for instance, that, say, characters from *The Aerodynamics of Pork* exist on the periphery of the lives of, say, characters in *Facing the Tank* or *Little Bits of Baby*. Is that true – or is it my imagination?

'I hate the idea of creating a character or a milieu then

21

discarding them as I move on. I like the idea that each of my novels is an expansion of a fictional society I've already set up. Thus there are mentions of the Peakes (*The Aerodynamics of Pork*) in subsequent novels, of Barrowcester (*Facing the Tank*), etc. The Trenellion Music Festival (*Pork*) – certainly the Cornish setting – may be cropping up in my latest. Iris Murdoch does this too – I think it's a pleasant reward for the faithful reader.'

Facing the Tank – recently out in paperback – has a structure that reminded me of Trollope and a style that could have come from M.R. James. Which writers have influenced you?

'Iris Murdoch is an ideal of mine. For all her prolixity (and her more recent works have been *very* big) I admire the way she confronts painful philosophical truths through the medium of social comedy. After all, this is how we stumble on such truths in real life – by falling in love, or being betrayed or watching a friendship die, or a friend – and at its strongest, fiction should be able to recreate such revelations; to provide comfort or confirmation.

'As for influences (as opposed to emulation) every English novelist writes under the burden of the great Victorian "three-decker" writers, George Eliot, Thackeray and co. I happen not to have fought against it. I was reared on Dickens, Trollope, Austen et al and they have left me with a delight in the elegant sentence or portentous phrase which is very hard to throw off. *Facing the Tank* (as much a homage to *Vainglory* as to the Barchester Chronicles) was in a sense a way of writing the Victorians out of my system while getting in a kick at the absurd rediscovery of "Victorian values." *Little Bits of Baby* I hope is pure Gale rather than school of somebody else.'

And which writers do you read?

'I'm an omnivore, which is why reviewing the very mixed bags of paperbacks for the *Telegraph* is such fun. It brings me guilt-free trash. Murdoch aside, I'd make a point of reading anything new from Tom Wakefield, Michael Carson, Candia MacWilliam or Shena MacKay. I'm only just discovering biography, largely thanks to

Rupert Christiansen's wonderful works on the prima donna and the Romantics. I can quite happily read Jane Grigson in bed; she has raised the humble recipe book to the level of High Art.'

As a novelist, do you not find reviewing fiction distracting?

'It's only distracting in that it takes up time I would rather be filling more creatively, but I find it teaches me a huge amount about fiction mechanics – why one story-teller might succeed with drab material where another can turn a golden idea into dross. I think there is something admirable about Jeanette Winterson's purity of approach in reading no contemporary fiction and doing no reviewing, but I do like to keep abreast of what other writers are up to (if only to avoid contributing to a vogue) and my work as a critic can stop my profession feeling so solitary.'

As a novelist, you appear to be rather optimistic – your books don't really have villains and, generally, things turn out for the best. Would you consider yourself an optimistic person?

'While I am profoundly cynical about most areas of public life, I do have a great trust in human potential. I go through life expecting the worst which means that I am pleasantly surprised at least once a week. I think that makes me an optimist. My continuing to vote Labour certainly does . . . '

There is perhaps a sourer note in *Little Bits of Baby* than in previous novels – though *Kansas in August* was set in a decaying inner city. Does this stem from a personal belief that things aren't quite so hunky-dory or simply because you're maturing as a novelist and your 'eye' is sharper?

'I don't think *Little Bits of Baby* is any sourer than *Kansas* was; if anything its various elements end by presenting a more hopeful view. The difference is that *Little Bits of Baby* is peopled by characters whom experience has taught to expect less, whereas *Kansas*, a fairly withering look at romantic idealism, gave most of its "air-time" to Dan and Sumitra, both of them hooked on sugary myths. I don't think my "eye" is becoming sharper but I am writing

23

longer novels about fewer people which evens the ratio of Gale's View to plot.'

Though the characters in your novels – on the whole – are from 'comfortable' backgrounds, they are essentially caring and – dare I say – inclined towards a socialist ethic. Certainly your venom in *Little Bits of Baby* is directed towards the get-rich-quick and grabby individuals. Do you find many contemporary attitudes depressing?

'I find what is happening in Britain deeply depressing. For want of proportional representation, I always cherished a naive trust in the tug-of-war in British voting patterns. Now I find that we've moved so far away from the democratic middle ground that in effect one side has "won" over the other and the complexion of our society has been ineradicably altered. Margaret Thatcher is so potent an ikon that when she makes a pronouncement, either directly against her detractors, or indirectly, via Clause 28 or DHSS cuts, a whole section of the population feels it has been given a moral dispensation to air views it might otherwise have thought indefensible. As a woolly liberal I find that frightening.'

Clearly Marcus – in *Little Bits of Baby* – is dying of AIDS. Why did you never designate it as such – or is it simply that as a gay man I have read Marcus's illness as AIDS?

'All that matters is that Marcus is dying. Our experiences of AIDS are forcing many of us to come to terms with our own mortality and the awesome fragility of our links to friends and loved ones in a way that has barely begun to happen to our parents. The process of mortality has been grotesquely speeded up but the complex of emotions that accompany it are the same. I touched on AIDS briefly in *Facing the Tank*, largely for the ironical Biblical imagery. At the moment the subject is too close for me to feel that I could treat it with any measure of control or without worrying about being exploitative.'

Musical themes seem to proliferate in your novels; why is this?

'Music is such an integral part of my daily life, whether I'm playing the piano, singing, whistling or just listening to the radio, that it would feel quite unrealistic to write a narrative without a "sound-track." Also, I'm an inveterate picker-out of lyrics; I love the haphazard way a song on the radio can become an ironic commentary on what's going on in a room.'

There is also a strong sense of the importance of religious belief running through your books; do you think faith important?

'Yes. But it needn't be anything to do with religion. I've tried to show in *Little Bits of Baby* how we're becoming a society without vision. I think it's vital to be brought down to size – by a belief in some supernatural power, or an encounter with someone's strength in the face of suffering, whatever – so that one can gain a wider view. Having church-going parents and having had to attend countless church services throughout my childhood and youth to sing, I find that the rituals and texts of Christianity are so deeply engrained in me that I cannot intellectualise my instant reactions to a Christmas carol, or a reading from St John. I'm not a church-goer but I am, shall we say, open to religious experience. If I had to answer strictly, I'd say I was a Buddhist with Pavlovian reactions of a Christian nature.'

I gather your sixth novel is already under way . . .

'Yes, it is. It's called *The Cat Sanctuary*; it's set in Cornwall and the cast is almost entirely female (of the men involved, two are dead and one has no genitalia.) It's a response to stories I've been hearing about abused childhoods. I had planned, as a challenge to myself, to write a book with absolutely no babies or religion in it but couldn't get beyond chapter seven without a funeral.'

You're now based in Cornwall. Why did you move out of London?

'I wanted a garden, wide open spaces, Atlantic air and so on. I love London but hated the way my friends and I would have to make appointments to see each other and then only briefly, exhausted from the effort and probably somewhere where we couldn't hear ourselves think. Cornwall is too far for people to come for the weekend so our friends come for proper visits and we have time for the sort of conversations most people had to give up in their early twenties. Now that I don't live there, I can treat my trips to London as usefully neurotic holidays – much healthier.'

Finally, what ambitions do you have for the future?

'To write convincingly about straight men – surely they remain one of the mysteries of modern society – and to write an adaptation of someone else's novel for television.'

Damon Galgut

'I've been writing since as far back as I can remember, but it really became important to me when I was twelve,' acknowledged twenty-five-year-old Damon Galgut, in Britain from his home in South Africa for publication of his collection of short stories, *Small Circles of Being*, and *Winter's Tales: New Series, 4* in which his short story *The Night of the Blood* appears. 'There was an English teacher at school who inspired me and showed me how exciting writing can be. He fired me with enthusiasm.'

Galgut's first published work – *A Sinless Season* – was a novel conceived when he was seventeen and published two years later. 'I wrote at night while playing classical music and burning jasmine incense,' he admitted. 'At first I thought I'd go crazy if anyone in the family made a noise, then I began to get involved and didn't mind so much any more. But it was heavy going, I can tell you . . .

'Without my knowledge, it was sent to a publisher by a friend and ex-teacher . . . '

When *A Sinless Season* was published in America in 1984, it was favourably noticed and compared with *Lord of the Flies*. *The Night of the Blood* and the short stories in *Small Circles of Being* show considerable skill – but they also exhibit an extraordinary degree of pessimism in a writer so young. Abiding themes include loss, death and relationships which will not survive. The title story – a particularly powerful and bleak piece – concerns a young boy who becomes critically ill and how, during the course of what could prove to be a terminal illness, his relationship with his parents disintegrates; their marriage is totally shattered. At the age of six, Galgut had cancer and was very close to death. Evidently he writes from close personal experience.

'All my writing is very rooted in personal experience. Even when the stories aren't directly autobiographical I always deal with personal issues – however obliquely. I'm not really objective enough about my own writing, but it's certainly true that I've started up with my own experience and it often does seem to me that there's a time limit on relationships.'

The Night of the Blood is a carefully observed and sexually taut study of two youths whose intense relationship is destroyed after affection topples over into a single instant of sexual contact.

'That story was written out of a strong personal experience; I was exorcising a great deal when I was writing *The Night of the Blood*. There's a great deal of bitterness in that short story, though I'm not sure if that's a good thing.

'But it's also a fact that a lot of writers have tortured psyches – that's one of the requirements. Certainly it's my experience that well-adjusted people tend not to be good writers. Really good writing has an edge to it, passion.

'*Small Circles of Being* was written with contained rage and – yes – it's based upon my own experiences when I was younger. But it's taken fifteen years for me to become sufficiently distanced from it for me to be able to write about it. After Hemingway had been shot (during the First World War), he had an experience of leaving his body – he wrote that that experience had touched him in a very special way and it affected him and his entire writing life. Writing about her suffering from cancer, Susan Sontag said that you can't come away from an experience like that without being changed in some way. Yes, you're different.'

And yet Galgut hasn't examined life in South Africa in his writing. Is there any reason for this?

'I think living in South Africa brings you into contact with very brutal realities and I think it will take me a long while to become sufficiently distanced to write about it. Those realities are too brutal, too close . . . and that's not a reflection of indifference on my part.

28

There's a moral responsibility in staying there; there's also a moral responsibility in leaving. The important thing is to be aware of that responsibility and act on it either way.'

Currently a full-time student at the University of Cape Town Drama School (he has had three full-length plays produced), Galgut is 'tinkering with something at the moment. I aim to take a lot of time off next year just to write. So I hope to be producing more than I have been. It's possible to live by writing in South Africa – I can live far more cheaply there than I could here.' Looking a little weary – he was recovering from a late night – Galgut gave a disarming grin. 'I've had the experience of living as a student with no income . . . so I think I'll be all right.'

Stephen Gray

The Pelican Café, St Martin's Lane – haunt of monied Bohemia ('I went on its second or third day of opening and have become part of the furniture since,' Simon Callow announced recently in *Time Out*.) Around us are actors, agents, publishers – faces familiar, if not exactly famous. We are seated at a table in a discreet corner and our conversation is slightly halting as the process of eating gets under way.

At the table next to us, two men earnestly discuss Boris Vian's *J'irai cracher sur vos tombes* (*I Will Spit on Your Graves*.) Momentarily, Stephen Gray – briefly in London from his home in South Africa for publication of his novel, *Time of Our Darkness* – is distracted. 'How curious,' he says. 'Vian's novel was a very distinct spur to my book; reading it some years ago made me wonder what I could do with a novel about inter-racial sex.'

Time of Our Darkness is a compelling, ironic and frequently moving examination of a black/white gay relationship under Apartheid. Surely the book must have come in for censorship in Gray's homeland?

'My usual policy is to have nothing to do with the censor,' Gray responds, as his wine and my mineral water arrive at the table. 'However, my publisher submitted the book prior to publication for the obvious reason that he wanted to know if the book could be safely imported into the country.

'The censor kept the book for four months before handing down a judgement that the book is "not undesirable." Yet there are an enormous number of restrictions imposed upon its sale: it cannot be sold to anyone under eighteen; it cannot be displayed in shops or libraries; it cannot be sold by mail order – all this is to avoid kids getting hold of it. This is painfully ironic – because it forces it to become an under-the-counter book sold in plain wrappers. The same set of restrictions apply to a book called *Sex for Teenagers* – which is only available to adults . . . And at the same time the government wipes out *fifty* black liberation documents.'

Is gay literature generally under threat in South Africa?

'There has been a spill-over there from gay publishing here and in America and until recently many bookshops had sections devoted to gay literature and these went unmolested. But in the past few weeks these have been closed down . . . and what was in the January issue of *Gay Times*? That's just been banned.'

Our food arrives and conversation becomes general as we set to. We talk about influences – 'I've learned a lot from books published by Gay Men's Press, which I try and read systematically. I'm a devoted admirer of Tom Wakefield's novels. Recently I've been reading a lot of Pavese . . . ' We talk about colonial literature – particularly that from Southern Africa (including Olive Schreiner's *The Story of an African Farm*, Nadine Gordimer, Athol Fugard, the rampantly heterosexual Roy Campbell "whose youth was interestingly homosexual" and William Plomer – a special passion whose work Gray is trying to get back into print.)

Talk about South African-born Plomer – a friend of Virginia Woolf and E.M. Forster and librettist for several Britten operas – brings us back to Gray's novel (his fifth, though the first for several years.)

Time of Our Darkness carefully delineates three basic sets of relationships: that between teacher Peter Walker and his Afrikaans lover André; that between Pete and Jenny – a British do-gooder whose actions create far more problems than they resolve; and, most importantly, that between Pete and Disley, a thirteen-year-old black African who has won a scholarship to the school at which Pete teaches and with whom he falls in love.

Was it Gray's intention – by focusing his novel on an

English South African – to write a novel in which the central characters served as a kind of microcosm of South African society?

'No, *Time of Our Darkness* doesn't have an allegorical meaning. I set out to write about a mixed set of characters who wouldn't normally mix socially. I wanted to underline more what people who don't meet socially have in common rather than their differences – *all* the characters in the book are forced to be socially outlawed.'

But what provoked Gray to focus his novel on gay relationships?

'It's not *entirely* about gay relationships,' he protests, 'though these are in the foreground. What it comes down to is the simple fact that all homosexual life is illegal in South Africa and I wanted to explore the Forster thing of connecting up. Normal black life is illegal – and I was puzzled that there is not a common bond. Why are black liberation and gay liberation in South Africa not aligned? White racism in South Africa shapes the common cause whites and blacks have – not gays only, but all liberation can be divorced from black and human rights issues . . . '

Peter, the central character, seems to have his head in the sand – he must know the situation, but doesn't appear to take any notice of it until it begins to affect him directly: is this generally true of individuals in South Africa?

'It's generally true of people – and of South Africans chronically so. I thought it a good vantage point to have at the centre of the novel a character who is forced to face things. But none of the characters is particularly representative. Each lives in his separate bubble. That's what South Africa is famous for: a society riven.'

By British standards South African gay society as represented in the novel seems very parochial.

'It's like a secret society, all very hush-hush and highly unpoliticised. *Time of Our Darkness* is set in 1985, since when gay people have become increasingly vocal, principally because there was a chance of law reform which rose to the surface and then sank again. We do have a magazine – *Exit* – which is a rallying point, but on the whole there is very little gay publishing. In South Africa there's a tiny press and publishing infrastructure, so writers are all-rounders. There are maybe half a dozen writers who are gay – two emerged recently, both Afrikaans – but they couldn't make a living from speciality writing. There's not a lot of gay writing – apart from things that are rather minor – because people just don't want to be arrested.

'But there's a tremendous interchange between writers. There's not a writer who is left-of-centre I've not known for years. The writer cannot be neutral. Serious writers have a lot in common with each other because we're all in an oppositional situation. Writers are called upon to make stands, make statements, lead workshops – you spend half your life doing that and then go home to write a book to back it all up. You can't be anything but an activist, committed in some way.'

But has Gray never felt a compulsion to move away from South Africa?

'In my youth I travelled; I was looking for another country, another life-style. I was privileged and lucky enough to be able to go outside and see – which is not the position of many South Africans in the arts. It's never far from the front of my mind – but South Africa's where I was born, where I must stay. I see a rotting of potential, a waste of human life, a criminal situation and have to work for something better and if I turned my back on it, I'd feel a terrible traitor.'

Joseph Hansen

'I think in all modesty that the really newsy thing about the Brandstetter books is that they actually found the readership necessary to make their continued publication practical,' admits author Joseph Hansen of his famous series of thrillers which feature a gay investigator of insurance claims. 'Back in 1967, when I wrote the first one, I never dreamed it would find a big, front-line publisher, let alone that eventually that book and the others in the series which followed would be kept continuously in print until this very day . . . not only in the U.S.A. but in Britain, France, Germany and Japan. That a sufficient number of mystery readers would care to read about a homosexual detective-hero, I doubt many people of whatever sexual persuasion would have believed, even in the optimistic sixties. Yet they did. And Dave's popularity continues to increase with each new title. It makes me feel fine, because I think readers are learning the simple lesson from these books that homosexuals are merely mortals much like themselves and hence entitled to the same consideration in life. I suppose someone else would have done this if I hadn't, but I'm grateful I was given the chance.'

With a string of successful thrillers which commenced British publication with *Fadeout* (1972) and continued through *Death Claims* (1973), *Trouble Maker* (1975), *The Man Everybody Was Afraid of* (1978), *Skinflick* (1979), *Gravedigger* (1982) and *Nightwork* (1984), Joseph Hansen has garnered critical acclaim and achieved healthy sales. 'It takes a genius to beat out a new literary form. Such a genius was Dashiel Hammett . . . In Joseph Hansen, it seems to me, Hammett has a worthy successor,' wrote H.R.F. Keating (himself a writer of thrillers of excellence) in a review in *The Times*. 'Joseph Hansen combines an intricate, well-machined plot with a superb evocation of the California scene,' applauded T.J. Binyon in *The Times Literary Supplement*.

Yet the Dave Brandstetter thrillers are but one area of Hansen's writing. He has also produced more straightforward novels of suspense which hinge on the sometimes frightening consequences of unconventional relationships. For example, *Steps Going Down* is about the obsessive love felt by an unsuccessful writer for a callow youth desirous of becoming a movie star: *Backtrack* follows the investigations by a seventeen-year-old into the life and mysterious death of his gay actor father, and this investigation all the while serves as a metaphor for his own journey into self-discovery. Though entirely contemporaneous, these novels are a part of an honourable tradition of writing about sexual tension and criminal intent which provided the whole basis for film noir.

You are probably best known for the Dave Brandstetter thrillers. Do you sometimes feel, like Conan Doyle with Sherlock Holmes, trapped by your most famous creation and, possibly, have a desire to kill him off?

'Dave himself would like to quit . . . except that he can't think what he would do with his time if he wasn't working. Yes, I sometimes get bored with him. He comes close to being shot to death by a Central American terrorist in the newest of his adventures, *The Little Dog Laughed*. But the terrorist is no virtuoso with his Uzi. He misses. And by now Dave is well into another case, to be called *Early Graves*, and slated for publication in the autumn of 1987. These days there is a demand for more Brandstetter books, so I'm writing them closer together than I used to. I liked to turn to another sort of writing in between – *A Smile in His Lifetime*, *Job's Year*, *Steps Going Down*. Now I take briefer breaks, in the form of novellas about a new detective character, Jack Bohannon.'

Did anything in particular inspire the Brandstetter thrillers and did you originally plan to write a sequence of tales about him – or was it rather the success of the first which propelled him into further literary life?

'Like a lot of novelists I started out as a poet, with a special liking for following set forms, the sonnet, the Spenserian stanza, and the like. I expect it was the rigidity of the form that appealed to me in mysteries, the challenge of working within tight and traditional limits. I had tried writing mysteries in my apprentice days, and thought it would be fun to give the toughest job in fiction to a homosexual, and this was how I came to write *Fadeout*, the first adventure of Dave Brandstetter. It amused me to make him an insurance death claims investigator, since the big American insurance companies have a notable aversion to homosexuals. There are many in-jokes in *Fadeout*, the turning on their heads of many unfounded notions the straight world harbours about us. I didn't intend to write about Dave again, but then it occurred to me (not a very practical man) that if I kept writing more books, readers might keep buying them, and eventually expecting and asking for more. This has turned out to be true. Dave is my bread and butter, bless his rather frigid heart.'

Was there any special reason which prompted you to locate the books in California rather than – say – Chicago or Denver or New York? Or are the books set in California because it's where you live?

'I came with my family in an old wreck of a car and about ten dollars left over to California from the cold and snows of the Mid-West in 1936, to live on a deserted fruit ranch in Altadena, where the deer came down the mountains to nibble the bark off the trees and peer in at us at night, their eyes glistening, their big ears alert and quivering. I've lived in Southern California since I turned thirteen . . . fifty years, in fact. I have set one novel in Wisconsin, one story there, another novel in New Orleans, and some stories and poems in South Dakota, but the bulk of my work is California-based, because I know the territory. I also love it.'

Your novels have a particularly strong sense of place; do you actually work from research and observation – for example, field trips to Venice for *Backtrack* – or from memory and imagination?

'I don't do research on my Californian settings. They rely for authenticity on my own observations. Jointly with a poet called John Harris, I ran poetry workshops in Venice from 1969 to 1974 and got to know the place well. The Venice of *Backtrack* is exactly as it was in 1970 when I wrote the novel (the book was a long, long time finding a publisher.) Now Venice is changing . . . the cottages are being bulldozed, and condominiums are rising in their place. I worry about what will become of the ducks.'

I feel that one of the abiding themes in your writing concerns cross-generalisation communications and problems – sexual and otherwise. Is this an area that especially interests you?

'It's true that we write about what preoccupies our minds, sometimes on so deep and hidden a level we need a stranger to point this out to us. At a guess, this business of kids and adults, young persons and middle-aged ones, figures in my work because I was a child of parents well into middle age, for starters. As a teenager I found myself attracted to men who I felt could teach me things about life and the world, art, music, history, politics. This often meant the men were older, didn't it? Sometimes not . . . sometimes they just knew things I was keen to know. But that probably explains something of the relationships in my novels. Then my wife and I raised one child of our own, and three kids we took in a little later . . . so I had some experience with kids underfoot that most homosexual writers miss out on, or are spared. It's a limitation to be able to observe and understand only oneself as a child, or at most oneself and one's sisters and brothers. I was lucky to have a steady companion in my wife. However rockily, we have stuck together for over forty years.'

I seem to remember that your earliest gay writing appeared under the pseudonym James Colton; what was the reason for this, and would you now publish any of those titles under your own name?

'One of my James Colton novels, originally published in 1968 as *Known Homosexual*, was republished in 1977 as *Strange to Himself*, and is now in print again, under the title *Pretty Boy Dead*. This was my first mystery novel, and its newest batch of readers seems to feel it is pretty good. When I re-read it in this latest of its incarnations, I thought so too. It has been published recently in a French translation, but no British publisher has yet picked it up.

'I began writing short stories for a Los Angeles gay magazine called *One* in 1961, and the editor there had an absolute rule that all writers for the magazine (except himself) must use pseudonyms. I argued against this in my case, but I lost. I was having a hell of a time getting my work published, and I decided it was better to publish under a pen-name than not at all. My stories as James Colton were popular, and when a book publisher took them on he wanted the Colton name on them, and after that, through eight novels, I kept the name. I only jettisoned it when a New York agent suggested I change it after he found me a first-rate publisher for *Fadeout* in 1970.'

I presume that your break-through in publishing terms came when you turned to the thriller form; what attracted you to the genre and were there any notable influences?

'The thing that decided me finally on writing in the mystery novel genre was reading the books of Dashiel Hammett, Raymond Chandler and Ross MacDonald. I felt these men were top-flight craftsmen, and that there was room in the form to say important things about men and women and how they cope with life. I have tried to deal with all sorts of social problems in my books while at the same time keeping the reader turning pages. With *Fadeout*, as I've said, I wanted to correct as many misapprehensions ordinary mortals have about homosexuals and the way they live as I could in the space of fifty thousand words. In *Death Claims* I dealt with a theme that has occupied me in more than one novel over the years . . . the obsession of a homosexual for an unattainable lover; I have seen this botch up many a life. I also dealt with the matter of drug addiction accidentally started by hospital treatment. In *Trouble Maker*, the character after whom the book is named is an unscrupulous lawyer exploiting young women by offering to collect overdue child-support payments from runaway husbands. And so on.'

Would you be interested in writing thrillers in which the main characters and situations weren't gay? If so, why? If not, why not?

'First, I am writing novellas or long short stories these days about a new detective, Jack Bohannon, who is not gay. He runs boarding stables on the coast, is a retired deputy sheriff, has an old ex-rodeo rider and a young novice priest as hired hands, and a wife who has retreated into mental blankness after being held hostage and raped by drug-runners on a fishing boat from Mexico. Bohannon's female companion is a young sheriff's officer named T. Hodges. I have done four long short stories about Bohannon, and plan to do another as soon as I finish writing the new Brandstetter novel. Five stories will make a book, and this will probably appear in the spring of 1988.

'For a very long time I had no interest in focusing my novels and stories other than on homosexuals. Why shouldn't I? There are more than enough straight novelists to look after that side of the business. But a magazine editor who has been very kind to me needed stories without a gay element for her publications, and I gave the idea a try, and found Jack Bohannon was pleasant company, along with his friends. We change.'

Why do you think that gay characters have been so consistently used as villains in thrillers – from Buchan (*Greenmantle*, I think) through Chandler and on up to the present day? And do you think that without gay liberation we would have had – or been allowed to have – thrillers in which the hero/detective is gay?

'People are frightened by what they cannot understand. Few people, including a good many homosexuals, can understand homosexuality: it frightens them; it repels them, and therefore writers with thoroughly conventional minds and attitudes naturally choose homosexuals to represent all that is contemptible and evil for their stories. This is no longer acceptable. I've written an essay on it in a book called *Murder Ink Revived* (1984). But I expect the habit

39

will die hard. Elmore Leonard, recently much celebrated in the U.S. as the best of thriller writers at work today, in a very recent book made one of the creepiest villains a homosexual . . . for no reason connected even remotely with the novel's plot-line.

'I think the sexual revolution of the nineteen sixties opened the way for writers like me to publish books that looked honestly at homosexuals and homosexuality. The freedom to print long-forbidden words helped. *Playboy* magazine helped. As for gay liberation by itself . . . I fear it led to gay segregation instead of integration, a turning inward instead of outward, and that its propagandising in favour of casual sex has had disastrous results.

'More serious and concerted efforts to change adverse public attitudes towards homosexuals and their life-styles were needed, as were dedicated and unremitting efforts to change the laws of this country that deny homosexuals equality with other citizens. Too much energy was filtered off into demonstrations of antic and captious nose-thumbing at the straight community that only reinforced its anti-homosexual bias. With the arrival of AIDS, the straight community (no matter that it piously pretends otherwise) basically believes the giddy, promiscuous, outrageous, and taunting gays are getting what they deserve, getting what they earned (if you please) by their so-called liberated behaviour. If I didn't think heterosexual attitudes could be changed, and dark minds enlightened, I wouldn't have written my books, and wouldn't go on writing them. I have hopes for the future. But I would feel more secure in those hopes if I thought others of my gay brothers and sisters were serious about gaining a fair and decent treatment by making some sort of effort beyond flouncing down the main street in tinsel costumes on Gay Liberation Day.'

Finally, do you consider yourself a 'gay writer' or 'a writer who is gay' and do you much associate with other writers from either category . . . or do you tend to work in a kind of isolation?

'I haven't had the luck to associate much with writers of any sort. Now and then I'm invited to conclaves of mystery fans where they can meet and audit panels of professional writers, but only once did I ever appear on a panel with other homosexual writers . . . and this was when the American Library Association (I think) invited Paul Monette, Daniel Curzon and me to speak, a couple of years ago.

'On rare trips to San Francisco I have encountered Curzon more than once, and have met a couple of other noted gay writers . . . but only fleetingly. I tend to think that writers for the most part don't make terribly interesting company for each other. I used to teach writing on the U.C.L.A. campus here, and bright-eyed aspirants often asked me, "What do writers talk about when they get together?" My answer was, invariably, "Money, contracts, agents, money, publishers, money, editors, money, advertising budgets, money, print runs, money, and, of course, money." Writing is a solitary business that makes Jack a dull boy.

'And to answer your first question, I am a homosexual, and I write largely about homosexuals because I believe I am able to do this with some accuracy, and can throw some light on a segment of our society that is poorly understood and badly treated.'

Patricia Highsmith

Graham Greene has described Patricia Highsmith as 'a writer who creates a world of her own – a world claustrophobic and irrational which we enter each time with a sense of personal danger. It is not the world as we once believed we knew it, but it is frighteningly more real to us than the house next door.'

Born in Fort Worth, Texas in 1921, Patricia Highsmith has lived in Europe for more than twenty-five years. *Strangers on a Train*, her first novel, published in 1950, was filmed in 1951 by Hitchcock and helped establish her reputation. 'It did help. It did linger and it did help that Hitchcock used the same title . . . which makes people remember it. But the film can't ever be remade, because the Hitchcock estate will not release the rights.' Since then Ms Highsmith has published eighteen novels and six collections of short stories; her twenty-fifth book, *Found in the Street*, will be published later this month; three of her books about amoral but utterly charming rogue Tom Ripley have just been reprinted in a compendium volume. Without any shadow of doubt, Patricia Highsmith is acknowledged as a master of tales of unease (the adjective 'thriller' simply won't do); yet the woman behind the brilliant and disquieting books is almost as mysterious as her talented Mr Ripley.

For all her years in Europe, Highsmith still possesses traces of a Texan drawl; penetratingly observant, she knows how to field an interviewer's questions and firmly believes that her private life is hers alone. When asked about memoirs or autobiography, she emphatically states that she has no intention of writing either.

Reviewers often categorise Highsmith's novels as 'thrillers'; is that how she views her books?

'Well, they're not always full of action. But to answer your question; maybe more than fifty per cent of my books have a murder in them. Yet I cannot call a book like *The Tremor of Forgery* a thriller because it's very slow and the only piece of action is when the hero throws a typewriter . . . and then it's dubious whether he killed another man or not. It's rather mixed. There's another word that's used – "suspense" – which I find rather boring, because I think *all* stories have suspense.'

If one were to trace the historical line of descent, the ancestor of Highsmith's novel would be the Dostoevsky of *Crime and Punishment* rather than the Wilkie Collins of *The Moonstone*. The workings of the mind (criminal or otherwise) seem to fascinate her.

'Yes, that's definitely what interests me. I usually go along with the murderer – not in the case of *Found in the Street* – but in most cases, so that people know the reason for the murder and they know what brings a person to do it. Sometimes, of course, the murderer is a bit cracked, insane . . .'

Does this imply that Highsmith is fascinated by murders?

'I'm interested in the guilt that follows murder or in the absence of it and I'm also interested in the procedure leading up to murder; the strain, or whatever it is, the events that create the circumstances that create the necessity to do such an act. I'm not obsessed with the violent act itself . . .'

In *Found in the Street* the murder is almost incidental; here obsession is the mainspring of the plot. The book commences when Ralph Linderman, an elderly man who hates what he sees as the corruption of the modern world (specifically, contemporary Manhattan), finds and returns to its well-heeled owner a cash-filled wallet. Linderman is already obsessed by a beautiful young girl, Elsie, who slowly comes into the orbit of the owner of the wallet and his sexually ambiguous wife. Linderman constantly spies on Elsie and on Jack Sutherland (owner of the wallet) and

Natalia (his wife), convinced that Jack is having a sordid affair with Elsie that is wrecking his (Jack's) marriage. Linderman does not realise that the all-appealing Elsie is actually having affairs with the various women with whom she lives throughout the course of the book. His obsession turns him from a harmless eccentric into a character of menace.

How did Highsmith get the plot for her latest novel?

'By jumps. For instance, I wanted to do the wallet idea because I've always wanted to find a wallet myself and return it . . . because I thought it would be a nice surprise for whoever lost it. But I never did, so I satisfied myself by writing the scene and then of course I had to build the rest of it. I also wanted to use the idea of an attractive individual, male or female, as seen by a couple of people . . . I wanted to have an eye-catching girl of the type that Marilyn Monroe was, the kind who turns men's heads, *anyone's* heads, I suppose. I wanted to create this simple girl who has the same power. Yet Elsie is not developed yet; her education's not finished; she's just beginning to mature . . . though of course, in my opinion, Marilyn Monroe depicted a completely empty-headed blonde; to me she's probably the sex object of a boy of eighteen . . . '

From Bruno, the psychopath killer in *Strangers on a Train*, to Tom Ripley in the four novels which chronicle his 'adventures', to Elsie in *Found in the Street*, sexually ambiguous or bisexual or homosexual characters have figured in Highsmith's fiction. Ripley, for example: he's the hero of the books but also the character who, in a way, the reader should morally disapprove of because of his actions. Is his sexual ambiguity used as some kind of comment?

'No,' Patricia Highsmith states. 'Only part of it is. Part of one of my theories is that a person who murders has something mixed up in his or her sex life and does not get a moral or even happy sex life. For instance, Peter Sutcliffe, the Yorkshire Ripper; there was something very odd about *his* sex life. In my opinion, he was impotent . . . and not a closet homosexual as Julian Symons suggested in his review of Gordon Burn's *Somebody's Husband, Somebody's Son*, the book about the case . . . There's something unsatisfactory about a killer's sex life. It just isn't there; he hasn't got an ordinary girlfriend or a wife.'

Yet Ripley is one of those people who – if he existed in real life – one would be fooled by, won over by, with whom one would go along with anything he suggested.

'I don't know whether it's possible to have a person like Ripley, unless he's in the Mafia, which I detest, just as Ripley does, someone who can be so cool about having killed something like seven people. Ripley is remorseful only about his first murder because he killed a friend and he did it for money.'

Ripley is undoubtedly Highsmith's most famous creation. Does she ever find herself in a Conan Doyle and Sherlock Holmes situation, thinking 'I'm expected to do another Ripley novel; perhaps I should kill him off'?

'No. If a good idea comes to me I'll write another Ripley.'

Is Ripley a character with whom Highsmith identifies?

'Yes. I think so. He's an expatriate who's decided to live in France. Of course, I don't identify with him because of his methods.'

And what about Highsmith's own methods? Though she has lived in Europe for so many years, her books set in the States possess an amazing accuracy of detail. Does she travel a lot for research?

'With *Found in the Street*, I went back first to look around with the idea of the book and then after writing the second draft I went back again to check. Within one year I went back to New York twice. I certainly don't mind travelling to check something out. It's possible to write a book in which you don't need the distances, but I'd rather see it. For instance, if Jack has to run from Grove Street to SoHo, I'd rather look at it than use a map.'

Is Highsmith a fast writer?

'I don't consider myself a fast writer. It takes about a year for me to write a book. I aim to write every day, but one can't always make it and sometimes one takes a trip for two weeks and when you come back it takes a week to settle down again. Also, I write practically three drafts of a novel and that's very time-consuming. I don't use a word processor; I haven't tried one – but I'm not inclined to like the idea.'

What provoked Patricia Highsmith to transplant herself to Europe in the first place?

'I'd been there on trips twice before, at one point for a year and a half, and I thought it would be more interesting than the States and I still think so. I like the architecture and the people and the languages and the values . . . Now I can do European scenes if I wish to, though I'm not so sure I could do a character, say, who was German by birth or education. I'm not sure. It's easy for me to put Americans in Europe . . . as I do with Ripley.'

Dorothy L. Sayers, Agatha Christie, Margery Allingham, Ruth Rendell, P.D. James, Patricia Highsmith, some of the most successful exponents of novels about crime and detection are women. Why?

'I have no idea. The only reason I can think of is that women are said to pay attention to detail, which can help if you're writing a mystery. But that's not a satisfactory answer. Certainly observation doesn't have anything to do with writing ability, nor does it have anything to do with creating plot. I don't know . . . '

Patricia Highsmith: a thoughtful quiet woman; intensely private, perhaps something of a gypsy – in her years in Europe, she has lived in England, Italy, France and now Switzerland. Patricia Highsmith: a brilliant writer of compellingly readable, often deeply disturbing novels about the pressures and psychological disturbances of contemporary life. *Found in the Street* is but the latest stunning example. Patricia Highsmith: as mysterious as her own Tom Ripley?

Alan Hollinghurst

Considering that so much of Alan Hollinghurst's first novel *The Swimming-Pool Library* is located in the murky basement swimming-pool of a recreational club that bears more than a passing resemblance to the Y.M.C.A., it seemed entirely appropriate that we should meet in a stuffy subterranean office at his publishers in the heart of Bloomsbury. So intense was the heat we might well have been on the upper reaches of the Orinoco.

By the time plastic beakers of tea had been served, we had removed outer layers of clothing and the sweaters beneath. At right angles across a conference table, we talked about the novel – an extraordinary piece of work which holds a reflecting glass up to both the recent and the not so immediate past. What makes *The Swimming-Pool Library* of such particular interest is the fact that Hollinghurst has elected to mirror a homosexual past – he describes this as 'trying to reclaim a past' – which captures fragments of time (rather like highly animated tableaux) from the early years of the century to the very fag-end of pre-AIDS gay London in the early eighties. It would be easy to describe the book as nostalgic, as an elegy for a way of life that has gone for the appreciable future – if not for ever.

But Hollinghurst has been motivated by something more than sheer sentimentality. On a directly personal level, he wanted to write a novel which encompassed the period between his birth – in 1954 – and more recent events which were significant but of which it was possible to be oblivious. 'It was my aim to write a novel about some of the things that had been going on in my country during my lifetime, but which it was possible to be unconscious of at the time – the first purges against gays in 1954, for example, or the early race attacks.'

The Swimming-Pool Library is an enormously entertaining novel which adroitly combines social observation, a finely tuned sense of history – and more specifically – a history of a specialised group and a wonderfully exuberant eroticism. The book is full of allusions – to Firbank (whose collected letters Hollinghurst was to have edited, before problems with a copyright holder aborted the project), to William Beckford (the hero's name – William Beckwith – and his ivory-tower existence are suggestive of the eighteenth-century eccentric), to Forster and Britten. One notable sequence – set at Covent Garden during a production of Britten's *Billy Budd* (first performed in 1951) – focuses on dilettante present (in the shape of William Beckwith), repressive past (in the shape of his wealthy grandfather, a former Home Secretary and instigator of purges against homosexuals in the fifties) and the continuity of things (relationships, creative achievement, as represented by Peter Pears – seen from their box by the hero and his grandfather.)

William Beckwith is a callow youth – though aged twenty-three; bronzed and beautiful; for ever working out at the gym or in the pool and for ever in pursuit of delicious young men, many of them black. 'He was very deliberately written as a rather heartless character,' Hollinghurst agrees, 'with no awareness of the past and little comprehension of the future. At one point I'd intended writing an epilogue which would have made it clear that William was "writing" the book practically on his death-bed with AIDS – but I forgot that idea because it was too much of a cliché. It would have been too neat and turned the novel into a moral fable.'

It is while cruising a cottage that Beckwith encounters – and saves the life of – the elderly Lord Nantwich, an old Africa hand who – to show his gratitude – suggests that he (Beckwith) becomes his biographer. It is by reading Nantwich's diaries that the hero begins to discover something of the history of his kind. Clearly this background was the result of research. 'I read a lot around the period, so that details were accurate – but I don't think research should show too much. I did far more reading about the Sudan – dry-as-dust memoirs by colonial administrators – to recreate the feeling of Africa.'

Firbank, a thread which ties together the past and the present, was chosen deliberately. 'I could have invented a novelist, but this was my way of doing my bit for Firbank,' Hollinghurst explained. 'I think he is an important writer with far more depth than many people acknowledge and his reputation has never become as firmly established as it should have done.'

Though *The Swimming-Pool Library* (the title reflects back to the hero's schooldays but could as easily refer to his use of the club's baths as a kind of library of men) is an affectionate evocation of period, and though throughout Hollinghurst has fully utilised the rich iconography of gay sub-culture (it is a book as much about bodies as it is about minds), it is not without subtle observation of the less acceptable aspects of gay life.

It is something of a truism to claim that homosexuality allows all those great divides – class, age, culture, background – to be bridged. Hollinghurst is aware, and it is implicit in his novel, that Beckwith's lovers (and those of others in the cast) are sex objects chosen for their race (black) or their class (working); that age is seen as a barrier to desire, and that culture, background, whatever, keep individuals firmly in their places. William's black lover is a toy soon tired of; Nantwich's Sudanese lover remains for ever a beloved servant; there is little cross-class conversation (body language is all) and true equality exists only between equals.

Beckwith moves through life with the sense of security available to the privileged classes – and when he is violently assaulted by a group of skinheads about whom he fantasises while visiting a working-class estate the shock is intense. His world will never again be quite so safe. Hollinghurst, who had a similar experience while at Oxford, agrees that once a previously unperceived threat is made apparent, one's view of the world is for ever changed.

Likely to provoke controversy, not least because of the explicit (though not gratuitous) scenes of sex, *The Swimming-Pool Library* is a novel of great richness – combining elements of an erotic detective story (and a particularly shocking denouement) with great wit and intelligence.

And what next? Hollinghurst, currently Deputy Editor of *The Times Literary Supplement* is planning a novel set in the country. 'Perhaps it sounds a little dull after *The Swimming-Pool Library*?' he queries. That seems most unlikely . . .

Timothy Ireland

There has been a gap of four years between publication of Timothy Ireland's *Who Lies Inside* – described by *Time out* as possessing 'an immediacy and freshness which capture perfectly the confused and isolated pain of adolescence, and in particular the special angst involved in the discovery of sexuality' and winner of the 1984 Other Award for teenage fiction – and his new novel *The Novice*, the story of twenty-three old Donovan Crowther, a virgin, just arrived in London and desperate for that happy-ever-after love affair.

'I originally conceived *The Novice* as a sequel to *Who Lies Inside*,' Ireland, a softly spoken twenty-nine-year-old, currently resident in Brighton and training to be a nurse, explained. 'I worked on it for a period of four years during which time it has gone from being a substantial novel telling three stories to a much shorter work concentrating on the one story. I had one lengthy gap of a year away from it which enabled me – when I returned to it – to be much more detached and ruthless when I was cutting and rewriting it.'

Surely he had set himself a difficult task, deciding to write a novel which centres on great expectations and which revolves around two essentially unsympathetic characters – Donovan and Davy, the older man he attempts to settle down with?

'It's fair to say that Donovan has these great expectations – but he is a novice because he has all these romantic views of a relationship and then finds out that it's not like that at all. Yes, it *is* hard to write about innocence, but I wanted to show that great expectations are not only true of experienced people but gay people in general who – I feel – do have inflated expectations. As soon as they meet someone, they want to move in together – they have a lot of illusions. Yet it's still quite difficult to form a compatible relationship; it's still quite difficult to meet friends. The difficulties and the underground nature of much gay life mean that when people do meet they expect an enormous amount very quickly. Because gay relationships are not overseen much by society, people make that lever of commitment very quickly . . . '

But isn't the outcome of *The Novice* rather pessimistic? After enduring Davy's infidelities and his essential inability to commit himself, doesn't Donovan look set to follow the same pattern?

'I wanted to show that the way you're treated can cause you very easily to fall into the same cycle of working as the people you've encountered. But indirectly I feel that Donovan *wasn't* going to become another Davy. He has got to take responsibility for his own feelings. If the book had carried on beyond the point where it ends, Donovan would have left Davy and perhaps begun something with Jimmy, the character he is becoming friendly with towards the end of the novel. I don't believe that lives are so ordered that we finish one thing and tie up all the loose ends before going on to the next thing – it seemed to me more realistic to end with an overlapping of Davy before going on to something else. It's not cynical – it's more like life; things need sorting out before you move on to something else. Of course, I'm aware that it's very hard to make Donovan sympathetic because I'm aware that most people reading about him will be more worldly-wise and thus likely to lose patience with him . . .

'And with Davy I wanted to draw a character who is unaware of how easily he can hurt his partner – in a way because such people do not take responsibility for their actions or for the effect of their actions. This is something gay people, particularly *older* gay people, are more prone to than heterosexuals. I wanted to show that you have to make a bit more effort and that with fidelity you make a conscious and deliberate decision. Infidelity is very upsetting for the partner – so saying it doesn't mean anything is an indefensible argument.'

With *The Novice* safely launched, what future writing plans does Ireland have?

'I would like to write a novel in which the central character is a woman. When I was writing *The Novice* I felt I wanted to write a novel in which the central character was not gay. I've written two novels now about characters who happen to be gay, though my first two books weren't gay at all. I'd also like to write a novel about loss, about picking up the pieces and about the inescapability of the past. The problems of re-ordering one's life – people think they can leap-frog from one experience to another, but thereby they create more problems for themselves. This would have to be written from an older person's perspective. I'm also considering a book based around AIDS issues.'

Christopher Isherwood

Durrants Hotel, near Baker Street, has that wood, pewter and brocade opulence that the English so delight in showing to foreign travellers as 'traditional.' The lobby is thick with carpets and American accents.

Among the guests is Christopher Isherwood who greets us quietly and hesitantly suggests that we talk in his bedroom, away from the babble of the public rooms.

It's a hotel bedroom like all hotel bedrooms, mirrors, teak veneer, and twin beds, one unmade and sportively rumpled. There it is that we begin by talking about Isherwood's latest book to be published here – *Christopher and His Kind*.

His frank retelling of *Goodbye to Berlin*, with all the sexual 'i's dotted and 't's crossed, has split the critics. Philip Toynbee told his heterosexual readers that there was plenty for them to learn in the Authorised Version of Isherwood's most famous novel. Dame Rebecca West waved an unaccustomed phial of sal volatile and exclaimed that it was nothing but a tale of the sordid exploitation of working-class youth.

Christopher Isherwood was by no means the first of his or any generation to be lured by the attractions of willing working-class boys – willing at a price. What was that attraction?

'I think in my case it was more anti-upper-class than pro-working-class. But there's no question that at that time there was something about the working class, something to do with D.H. Lawrence, a feeling that the working class had a dark centre whereas other people didn't have a centre at all.

'They had a great instinctive warmth, and you felt on a more human physical level with them. I used to feel that upper-class boys were a little bit untouchable and unphysical. We were all hard collars and a little bit tight somehow. It all had to be loosened up.

'Later it changed, and when I came back to England from Germany I found really that there was not all that much difference, though I felt attracted to people who had some kind of physical expressiveness. Dancers, for example, who are loosened up just by putting their feet on the bar every morning – they are also loosened up psychologically in consequence. And I think that I eventually loosened up considerably as well. I really took to it.

'It's true I didn't have very many sexual experiences at that time, though of course I was going to bed with Auden a lot. But there were people who cropped up in increasing numbers. Everything was different after I had been to Berlin. It was as though I had discovered how. Immediately I came home I started picking people up left, right and sideways, and all this business with the working class – and all that jazz – suddenly was irrelevant. I would make do with people I met at cocktail parties just as well.

'And of course one changed physically too, because screwing a lot makes you more attractive. It shows somehow. I was very shy at first, thought I was very unattractive. A lot of people are like that. Then I started realising that I could get a lot of people and so that helped.'

Your friends have always been rich sources of material for your writing. Do many object to being characterised in print?

'I've always made no bones about it if I write something which refers to somebody. I've always just sent it to him, or her, and said: "Look, one word from you and we'll throw the whole thing in the fire." Of course that's bluffing a little bit, but in fact I was almost taken up on it a couple of times by people who really felt they didn't want something printed. But in the end it turned out all right. You know, people rather enjoy being in books. It's not basically offensive – it is a great act of interest and

55

affection to want to write about somebody and, as I always used to say, I never write about people I don't like. They bore me.'

Can we take an example – Gerald Hamilton. How did you make use of him as Mr Norris?

'All the beginning part about Gerald is more or less faithfully recorded. The only thing was that, rightly or wrongly, I chose to introduce this rather melodramatic plot, and towards the end of the book I got in the grip of the plot and even lost Gerald for a little while because we had those sensational scenes in Switzerland which were simply just invented.

'But in general all the mannerisms and the way Gerald talked are exactly reproduced. It's interesting; the way somebody talks is like a foreign language. After you have mastered the elements of it you can start talking it for yourself. So I could write dialogue in his manner. It is very easy to imitate most people's speech patterns because they don't vary. One has favourite words and turns of phrase that one uses.

'Basically, the invention with Gerald consisted in his having this kind of familiar sinister secretary. I daresay he did have some sinister secretaries, but there was never anyone quite as faithful as the character in the book who pursued him in that sort of way. However, he did have a kind of business that was rather nebulous – just like in the book – and he did have an apartment rather like that, and there were always bailiffs and people lurking in the background. So a lot of it is reportage.'

And then presumably he became Mr Norris for the rest of his life?

'Well, he took to it rather – yes. After the initial protests. It was impossible not to be charmed by Gerald Hamilton. All kinds of people with very clear-cut codes of morals nevertheless liked to spend time with him because he was so very entertaining.'

You are best known for your stories about Berlin. Do you ever feel shackled by those books?

'Quite obviously, when you have been attached to anything as famous as this *Cabaret* film, however indirectly, that does mean that far more people know you for that reason than for any other. But it doesn't faze me at all – I have a lot of healthy self-esteem and I am quite able to go ahead and not worry. I know that according to my values some of my later books are far superior to the Berlin books.

'In fact it came to a real crunch the other day because I was recording some stuff for a record in the States, reading from my work. I thought – well, we have to have a bit about Sally Bowles. So I read this stuff. Now unless you are an actor the question of impersonation can be quite a difficulty, so there was a problem from that point of view. But as I was reading it I thought – how thin this stuff is. Then I got on to reading something out of *A Single Man* and that was ever so much better. It had more substance.

'When you are reading aloud you really do judge something very objectively because you know whether you can perform with it or not. Finally I read something I had written which you have probably never heard of in a little book called *Exhumations*, which came out in the sixties. It was about a bad trip taking hashish. And I realised that here was real substance – the other thing was too coy, too thin. I was not involved in it sufficiently. I was somehow playing with my cards very close to my vest – at least, that is how I felt.'

Did any of that enter into your decision to write *Christoper and His Kind*? That you wanted to get back to that time and produce an account with more substance to it? Or was it essentially an attempt to put the record straight?

'As a matter of fact I never intended to write *Christopher and His Kind* at all. I was going to bring out my diaries. But I thought I had to explain first why I came to the States. Thinking about it I came to the conclusion that from the moment I made the first move to go to Germany, and in view of everything that was in store for me like Hitler, the mess-up with Heinz's papers, and so on, everything kept steering me towards the States.

'So I thought I would write a little introductory chapter to tell all about that. Then I realised that I had a tremendous mass of material, a lot of it well worth recording, particularly the stuff about other people like Stephen Spender and Auden and other friends. And so what began as a short chapter turned into this relatively long book.'

And do you plan to carry on with an account of your later life in America?

'Yes, I'm going to continue with America, but I'm not going to bring out the diaries as I originally planned. For one thing, it does not matter whether I am alive or not when they are published. It is true I could annotate them, and I would cut them because there are about three hundred thousand words, but basically they are done.

'What I want to do at the moment – because it challenges me so much more – is to write about a Hindu monk whom I met shortly after I got to the States, and with whom I had a guru-disciple relationship from 1939 until he died in 1975. I want to write about it all in an extremely secular, novelistic, psychological way so that it does not matter whether you believe any of the religious stuff. I want to do it without sentimentality, avoiding everything like that, but somehow getting the essence of it, and I don't know whether I can do it.'

How did that relationship develop?

'When I met him I was at a point in my life when I was very much on the look-out for some new kind of direction. It also had a great deal to do with Anglo-Indian confrontation in a funny kind of way. Although I was a strong anti-Imperialist I was nevertheless the child of Imperialist Britain. I had been to public school; my father was in the army, and I had this inherited guilt towards India and all those other places. Now the Swami, before he became a monk, had belonged to a terrorist organisation against the British. So we were really confrontees and this, of course, led as it so often does to a strong mutual liking.

'I had immediately told him I was gay, the first time we met. I thought, well, let us see what this man is all about, because he was obviously by his nature totally or almost totally heterosexual.

'He was admirable about this. There was absolutely no question of his "patronising it" or anything like that.

58

He kept saying to me again and again all through our relationship, "Mr Christopher, the trouble is that you have this Western puritanism. You must not think in those terms."

'You see, he could understand that however "liberated" you are, and however you just carry on, there is still this awful, awful puritanism built into one. One is still surprised that people aren't shocked. For him it was nothing. It was like the old Jewish joke: "Oedipus schmoedipus, so long as the boy loves his mother . . . " It's another view of humanity, this understanding about love. We repeat these things, and yet all these words, words . . . if we could really get rid of all that shit, our enemies would be unable to touch us. We should convert them.'

Do you have a positive sense of fighting Western puritanism in what you write?

'Yes, yes, I have a sense of fighting it all right, and there is a lot to fight, especially back in America, my goodness. Some of the states are really appalling in their persecution of gays. Not just losing your job, which is quite bad enough, but people being beaten up. A boy was killed the other day.

'California, where I live, is an extraordinary state, absolutely split down the middle. It is a scene of almost unending battle on all subjects. The heavies, the conservatives, fight us liberals on every front. It's almost metaphysical – there are enough people on both sides so nothing can really happen. It's like a way between heaven and hell – it just goes on and on . . . '

With people like that police chief Ed Davis . . .

'He's like something out of Dickens, an extraordinary character. I sometimes wonder if he is not just camping it up – he carries on in such a way that you think it is an act. And perhaps he does not really dislike homosexuals. It is rather like some of those Nazis whom you suspected of not being anti-semitic but who just did it as an act. Just for fun. Which, of course, is the most hellish thing of all – to act like that even without hate.'

But this behaviour can be seen everywhere, can't it? There is a thrill in acting out one's beliefs, dramatising them. Take gay people. A good number of them are quite content to be gay and go happily and quietly about their daily lives. But a large number feel the need for the additional excitement of political action, demonstrations, even publishing gay newspapers!

'Of course – it's wonderful to have something to be aggressive about. Tactically speaking we all have different roles to play. My role is extreme respectability, old age, all that jazz. Other people use other methods. One uses what weapons come to hand. And I am really interested in what I try to do – appearing in quite serious academic gatherings and not screaming and waving the flag, but just laying it right down on the carpet for them to look at. And doing it rather casually in the middle of a speech about something else – that is also part of the battle.

'If you can get people to think that you know something, you can tell them what it is you want them to know.'

Don Bachardy, your lover – is he involved in this sort of work with you?

'No, not actually. As far as our life together is concerned, we lead very quiet, busy lives – painting, writing up a story, watching television and so on . . . and we lead a very nice gay social life. In Los Angeles there's an enormously big dance hall called Studio One where anybody can dance any night. And if you like seeing folk, there they all are.

'San Francisco is much better in a way because gays are very well organised, much more of a political force. People are really reckoned with and politicians think twice before clouting them.

'I had difficulty in believing this but there are parts of San Francisco where gays predominate. There are actually more of us. They have bought all the houses – and of course exactly the same thing is brewing against them as against the Jews.'

Why do you think that so many older gays now are making their statement at this point in their lives?

'It's an interacting process. It is all very well to say "make a statement" but then you need a mechanism to make it. With the emergence of the gay press, and a far greater coverage of gay issues, it becomes possible to make a statement and really be heard by a lot of people.

'I do think there is a kind of trap – which I fell into in the middle part of my life. I was living very openly as a gay and it did not really occur to me that you should make an explicit statement. Of course, the things I wanted to write dealt very often with homosexuality, but they did not necessitate, did not demand from a purely artistic viewpoint, a statement.'

Was a statement not needed in *Lions and Shadows*?

'Well, of course, that's the point – that's something else. Now that was a question of just being really scared to do it, I think. I thought it would rock the boat, upset the family, upset everybody. I don't see any defence for that. That was when it should have been done, and why the hell not? It would have been all right. One could have made a statement of some sort.

'It detracts in some degree from the book, and there is no reason why the book should have not been woven out of the same cloth as *Christopher and His Kind*.'

Did America prove to be your sexual homeland?

'Yes. There were a couple of people there, even before I met Don, who were just what the doctor ordered. We don't have a classless society in America, but we do have a middle class which practically wipes out everything else. It may be so in Britain – I am woefully ignorant about present-day Britain – but there is a sort of "thing" in America. You can go anywhere, in a garage, in a filling station, and you never know who you are talking to. You can find a philosophy major working in a garage – just another husky boy doing his thing. And there isn't that feeling that it is impossible for anybody to be doing anything.

'I see an enormous number of college kids – really the social group I'm most completely at home with in America – and I'm not just talking about gays but young Americans of both sexes from around eighteen to thirty. There is an enormous rapport, and there is something wonderful, great expression, kids with flowers kneeling in front of the National Guard with their guns. You almost feel they could lead a great crusade.

'A lot of them come to the house, or just call up from all over the place. I get into long conversations with them on the phone. I see a lot of them going through those terrible hang-ups – it's difficult for me to remember what those hang-ups were like. And they often bring them to me. It is no use giving them pious maxims on how to live their lives, no use telling them a lot of over-optimistic stuff. I just try to be myself as much as I can, and they say, "It didn't kill him so maybe I'll get through it too." It's all you can say really. But I get quite involved with them . . . destiny somehow.'

What made you finally settle in Los Angeles?

'That was largely happenstance, and the funny thing was it was almost entirely with non-Americans. First of all it was very important to me that Gerald Heard and his friend Christopher Wood were there. Both are dead now, but they were out there with Huxley. Now at the time I had reached a tentative position on pacifism and I wanted to talk about it to Huxley who had just brought out an important book called *Ends and Means* about the pacifism question. So that was a motive for going there.

'Teddy Roosevelt or somebody said that California is beyond the West – the real classic West is the mountain states, Arizona, Colorado, Utah, Nevada, Wyoming – then beyond that is California, the littoral. I thought that was romantic and I wanted to go out there.

'And after I got there, what did I do? I got involved with a Hindu monk, dozens and dozens of German Jewish refugees who had always been my tribe in a way because we all left Germany at the same time and I kept meeting them in Paris or Brussels or Amsterdam. They are not actually mentioned in the book very much because there were so many of them that you would have to go into a whole separate thing about them, but the refugees were really built into my life for the next ten years. You see, when the war situation developed I got involved with the Quakers and went east to a place outside Philadelphia where there is a sort of centre for Quakers. There was a refugee hostel and I worked there for the best part of a year. I was absolutely plunged up to the neck in the refugee thing again. So you see there was a very non-American side to my life all through this period.'

How long did it take you to become an American and take up with the American community?

'It was very gradual. A significant thing was that when I had been there for about ten years people began to say, really Chris, you've got such an American accent. And when I used to come over to Britain people in shops would say, "Over for long, sir?" They never say that now. As soon as I was at my ease my British accent came back, and I realised that I had been trying to adapt. People who feel at home in a country never bother about things like that. I remember coming into New York harbour on a ship one time, and this guy turned to me and said: "Der voss a lot of alienz on board . . . " He was simply some Pole who never bothered a shit whether he could speak English or not. From this point of view he was an American.

'And now, of course, the Spanish have so imposed themselves that it is getting alarming. We have bilingual notices in Los Angeles. I do hope there aren't going to be a whole lot of different languages. Communication is quite bad enough as it is.'

Did you start working in movies early on in Los Angeles?

'I had to. That was the only way I knew how to earn my money. How did I get job in the movies? Because I was in with all those refugees – and some of them were not at all refugees: I mean they found nooks for themselves very easily. Practically my first producer was one of Max Reinhardt's sons, Gottfried, who had a job at M.G.M. We made a couple of pictures together and so I got into the trade that way.'

Hollywood must have been extremely frustrating for creative writers, most of them having hardly any control over the films they were working on.

'Yes, it was. Ideally one should be writer/director. There's no other way of doing it. Even so, you are the subject of the most fearful pressures. You have to be such a politician to function, just to go up against the front office who are often totally ignorant people. They are businessmen who have come out from New York and know nothing about movie-making. No, it is very frustrating, that is true. But it is a funny thing. Quite aside from having money, you can enjoy the fun of plotting these things and putting them together so much that, although you feel pissed off when they never make the picture, or make it all wrong, nevertheless you have had a kind of fun. The reward is in the doing it.

'Sometimes, of course, we have done some really nice things. They don't always louse it up. So often it is simply that they don't have the funds and the whole project falls in the water. Don and I have taken to doing them together now. Tony Richardson asked us to do a script of *I, Claudius* and *Claudius the God* and we got a real nice script. We did another one with Tony which he abandoned later because of financial reasons – a script of Carson McCullers's *Reflections in a Golden Eye*. Then John Huston took it over and made his own script which he always does. But I think our script was better because it was written in absolute continuity. The story is full of flashback, but we started at the real beginning when the soldier spills something over the Major's uniform, and everything from then on happens in sequence. I can't tell you how much better it was that way. More organic.'

What attracted you to *Frankenstein*, which you did for Universal Studios?

'Oh, we were asked to do it, that was all. I love being asked to do legends, and I think we had a few good ideas, but they mucked it up so. It was the second half of it which was so brutally chopped about, and the producer and director wrote in whole scenes. There were moments in it when it was terribly lacking in style. For instance, we wanted to show the sort of roughness of a hospital in the early nineteenth century. Here was this boy who was to have his arm amputated. Now the great thing is that the surgeon just saws it as fast as he possibly can. A good surgeon was one who could do it very quickly. Meanwhile you were given some liquor as an anaesthetic. So there was this whisky bottle, and when the operation was all over the people who brought the boy asked, "How much do we owe you, doctor?" and he says, "Just give me what is left in the bottle." Now the next scene, according to us, was that Frankenstein and the doctor, who later turns out to be his instructor in body-making, are sitting on either side of the fire in the hospital passing the bottle back and forth between each other and drinking out of it. It gives an extremely physical sense, with all these people drinking out of the same bottle. So what does our director do? He has a table between them, and two glasses! It just destroyed the atmosphere of it. It was incredible. Little punches like that which are simply lost. It was more like a café – there they were with these glasses pouring out little, little nips.'

In your scripts for *Cabaret* you had the Christopher character totally heterosexual.

'Yes. It seemed to be all fun and games; I didn't find his homosexual duality organic at all. It was just a caprice, just to be naughty. And under the circumstances, in the particular period which *Cabaret* deals with, I found that a terrible put-down. "Ugh, it's so decadent, and what I won't do next, y'know. I've got a touch of homosexuality." It's as though it were flu or something.'

When *Cabaret* was shown on American television they cut the homosexual bit – which made even more nonsense of it, because nobody knew what was going on there.

'Yes. Michael York is fearless about it all, though. Did you see that picture called *Something for Everyone* where he commits the murder? He kissed that boy with the greatest aplomb.

'Michael is a very good actor. I thought he was awfully good in *Cabaret*. But most of the time in that film it's difficult to know what it is all in aid of. It's just people behaving. One thing we wanted to do was make the Joel Gray character, the Master of Ceremonies, a lodger in the house. He would have been a very mousy little man, almost invisible, and also, specifically, a Jew. He would have been beaten up by the Nazis, just enough to give him a fury, a hatred underneath. And then we wanted him to do what one of the great Jewish cabaret people actually did. This man was trapped in some way, knew he could

65

not escape, knew he was going to be arrested. So what this real-life star did was to get another comic to come on stage. And as the other comic comes on, the star gives him the Nazi salute. "What does that mean?" asks the comic. "That's how high the shit stands in Germany today," the star answers. After which they dragged him off and put him to death or something. There was a man so angry that he wanted to make his own personal statement.'

And what personal statements do you feel that you need to make?

'I feel I'm gay, that's very clear. My Hindu thing is my own affair – I am certainly not someone to go round trying to convert people. Those are the central facts of my life. I feel committed to liberalism, or whatever you want to call it. Or to civil liberties in a way, but mildly. I don't want to pose as leader in that way. I'm a figurehead, not a leader. It is for other people to declare you a figurehead. I just try to oblige, that's all, and get on with the job. There is plenty to be done, that's for sure.'

From the point of view of a figurehead, if not a leader, you must have your own feelings about the way gay people around you should best be working to end the sort of position they find themselves in?

'That's frightfully hard to answer because it's a question of individual attitudes. First, our right is to be free. And our function is to make a thing out of it. Our way of life has so much to teach the heterosexual majority. In many ways there is a greater relaxation, more simplicity about it. I don't like the idea of gay people having legal forms for their relationships, but it is impossible not to regret that you can't have, for instance, communal property. It's a very real problem, that. I don't know about this country, but in the States you run into things like gift tax if you try to share your money, and you have to resort to tricks to get around it – like adoption. That's why people get turned on by the idea of gay marriages.

'But that is something I don't like – the idea of swearing to be true. Just *be* true, and when you stop being true then that is perfectly all right too.

'In other words I think that a relationship can only exist

66

from moment to moment. It's no use promising this, that or the other. All kinds of relationships, unless they are between a pair of cows, are extremely bumpy affairs over a long period. It is just a question of adjusting to someone else and loving each other sufficiently so that the failures to adjust don't matter. But I haven't answered the question at all, of course, because I really don't know.

'I do believe in solidarity, because I don't want to see splinter groups forming, and that is why we must put up with things that we don't like to some degree.

'For instance, take our paper in California, *The Advocate*. It has this enormous section called *Trader Dick's* which is full of ads for erotica – for sex tools of various kinds. It makes that old Berlin scene look so innocent. Stuff which used to belong in a torture chamber, or in the Tower of London, is now sold to suburban couples to use on one another. Screamingly funny. But one must absolutely accept all of that somehow and not get "dainty."

'There are some people in Los Angeles who are anxious to challenge the community by being scandalous. I have great sympathy for that in a way. In the end one gets down to the question of tactics. You have to be cool about it and say, well, there are these tactics and the question is, will they work?

'Of course, we are completely without leadership at present. If somebody was planning the moves, if we were organised in that way, we would have great political power.

'But there is this eternal clash between the political power – the aggression which is necessary and which we need to carry through – and the other thing which is just saying why can't we all love one another. You are in a perpetual paradox.'

Francis King

After years of globe-trotting, novelist and critic Francis King has settled (for how long is anyone's guess) in a quiet Kensington back street. It was there that we called on him. We climbed the steps to the front door, rang the bell and waited.

After a few seconds the door opened and all hell broke loose. Never have two interviewers received such a warm welcome. This energetic little body simply flew at us from out of the shadows, hopping up and down with excitement, and nearly bowling us off our feet in his enthusiasm.

Then he started licking us.

'That's Joe,' said Francis half-apologetically, 'my bull-terrier.' Joe rounded us up and shepherded us into the narrow hall, between walls clogged with aquarelles, Japanese prints, and pen and ink drawings. A cat fled before us while Joe pursued us into the living room, still making like a whirling dervish. It was in this room, after a lunch of gin and chops, and under the imperious gaze of a bust which bore only the most tenuous resemblance to its owner, that we began to talk.

Had you always wanted to write?

'Yes, I'd always wanted to be a writer. At school I did a great deal of writing. And for a homosexual it's something that's very useful to do. Certainly when I started out you were under pressures if you did an ordinary job. But I think that as a writer you can be much franker about yourself and live much more freely.'

When did you begin your writing career?

'I started at school writing poetry – I think that's what

68

most people start with in adolescence. Then I went to Oxford and started on this book of mine *To The Dark Tower* during my first period at Oxford when I was 18 or 19.

'By the time I went up to Oxford the war had started, and I had to have a tribunal as a conscientious objector. There was this group of people – one of them Professor of Law at Oxford University – and a very sympathetic judge who was very nice indeed and very polite.

'He asked me when I first started being a conscientious objector. So I said, when I was fourteen I refused to join the Officers Training Corps. He refused to believe that – that any boy of fourteen would refuse to join the O.T.C. because he was a pacifist. So I said well, there's a letter here from my housemaster which says so. He asked me who my housemaster was, which school, and I said Shrewsbury. Now he in fact was a governor of the school so I think he was rather embarrassed by having doubted my word, and he exempted me from service on the condition that I worked on the land. Which was what I did.

'What was very interesting on the land, and something which I tried to bring up in *A Game of Patience*, was that I never had any unpleasantness from the people I worked with on farms. Very often they used to say to me, "If I had your brains I'd be a conscientious objector, but I wouldn't know what to say to the tribunal." A lot of farm-workers used to say that to me. The gentry were always very nice.

'The people who were unpleasant were the shop-keeping people. I'd go into the shops, wait till I was next to be served, and if someone came in after me they would very pointedly serve the other person first to show their disapproval. There was a little restaurant where I used to go and eat, and they always made a great point of keeping me waiting a very, very long time. Of course, I was young and nervous then. Now I'd say, "Look, why the hell am I not being served?" But in those days I'd just sit there waiting. There was this kind of small irritation which wasn't of any importance.

'I read a great number of books, which other people of my age wouldn't have had time to read, because there was nothing else to do. So I accumulated a great bank account of things I'd read – which was a great advantage.

'On the other hand, when I went back to Oxford, I was absolutely astounded by how sophisticated and worldly people were in comparison with myself, because they'd been through the war, they'd travelled; lots of them had been in Italy; they'd been in the Desert Campaign; they'd been in Germany after the war, and they all had this much greater sophistication. And in that respect I felt I was on a par with the people who had just come from school. On the other hand I'd read far more than most of my contemporaries, so there were advantages and disadvantages.

'This was really why I decided to go abroad. Suddenly I felt that I'd been boxed up, not only in England but for most of the time in the country, so I had this terrible craving to go abroad and immerse myself in experience. This is really what took me to the British Council. It's a very good career for anyone who wants to be a writer, certainly in the opening stages. You go abroad, you mix with all sorts of different people, and it wasn't too arduous when I first joined. One worked nine to five and had a lot of time for writing – it was well paid, and it suited me very well.

'One of the difficulties, though, was that as you became more senior you had to do much more entertaining. In some cases it was rather difficult if you didn't have a wife and a natural aptitude for running the house and organising parties – though some of the homosexuals I knew in the Council did it far better than Council wives.

'As employers, the British Council were extremely tolerant at that period when a lot of employers weren't. They were very civilised in their attitude provided you didn't make a scandal and provided you weren't too overt. Senior people in the British Council must have realised that I was a homosexual, but provided one didn't have a scandal they didn't hold it against one. It didn't prevent one from being promoted and getting jobs, whereas I think a lot of other organisations, business organisations, would have made it much harder. When I first went abroad with the Council I flung myself into every possible experience. I had a year and a half in Italy, then I went to Greece. Now, unless you're either very beautiful or very rich – and I was neither – it's very rare to be able to live out all your fantasies. But at that period in Greece you could; anything you desired you could find. So I had this period of extreme promiscuity, which was very exciting, and I think it's very good for everyone to go through that sort of experience. But when I went to Japan I settled down and quietened down, because I felt that I'd experienced all that. The strange thing in Greece was that it was a kind of Dead Sea fruit – you'd meet one very, very beautiful person after another; it all seemed marvellous, and yet it was all totally meaningless in the end.

'I had one friend who was very attractive, Greek, and I think he was genuinely fond of me. But it wan't love on his side. We had really very little in common. It wasn't until I went to Japan that I did meet someone with whom I had a great deal in common, who was also very attractive, a charming pleasant boy – very nice to go around with. That was when I settled down and gave up the promiscuous sort of life I had been leading.'

Was there a well-organised gay scene in Greece then?

'At that period there were absolutely no gay bars. There were no gay clubs as there are now in Athens. But simply anywhere you went . . . you only had to go to the beach, or walk through town. If you didn't speak Greek it was a barrier. But if you spoke Greek as I did it was the easiest thing in the world.

'And there was virtually nobody who was unobtainable – it was quite extraordinary. Admittedly money came into it because they were very poor – why shouldn't it? – but it was a very small sum of money, the equivalent of fifty p now. If they got the equivalent of a pound they thought you were being enormously generous. You'd go on the beach; you'd see somebody beautiful and you'd walk up and speak to him and as likely as not he'd be only too delighted to come back with you. It was all as easy as that.

'But because it was so easy, and this may have been part of the reason, it all seemed rather flavourless after a while. After seven and a half years of a life of extreme promiscuity

71

I felt I didn't want it again, which is why now I don't lead that sort of life. I like going to a gay bar or a gay club from time to time, but I don't go with the purpose of picking anyone up.'

You actually came to your homosexuality via a period of bisexuality.

'Yes, I was terribly late. I think this may have been because of living in the country, a sort of immaturity.

'I had a period of sleeping with women when I was working on the land. Didn't do it very often; didn't enjoy it at all. It was supposed to be something I was obliged to do. Then at Oxford there was a great deal of homosexual chatter, but in fact nothing happened, and it wasn't until I had my first job when I was well into my twenties, and I went to Venice and – the most hackneyed thing possible – I met a gondolier!

'Of course nowadays it would cost a fortune to go to bed with a gondolier, but I remember that he took me out in his gondola, and this is how it first happened. I realised then what I enjoyed most, and from then onwards bisexuality faded out and I became exclusively homosexual. It was very late and people are always amazed when they ask, "When did you have your first homosexual experience apart from rather elementary kinds of sex at school?" and I say it wasn't until I was about twenty-four or twenty-five that I first had proper sex with a man.

'I always feel rather sad about that because before that I can remember two or three occasions when I had what were obviously passes and I was terribly nervous and frightened, and withdrew. I think what one regrets in life are not the things that one did but the things one failed to do.

'I can remember when I was working in the country there was a farm labourer who was extremely attractive, and now I realise that he wanted to do something, but I repelled him and became very chilly when I thought this was what he was up to, and I always regret this now.'

You said earlier that the British Council didn't take exception to gay employees so long as they didn't cause scandal, but you were very discreet in your writing.

'I'm not sure that the fact that one couldn't be explicit was

72

not to a certain extent an advantage. This having to find a metaphor for one's own situation, which is obviously what Henry James did and what Maugham had to do, might have been a stimulus to the imagination. The fact that you had to seek for this metaphor in a different situation – a heterosexual situation – in order to express your own homosexual concerns was very often an imaginative spur.'

It was a long time before you could be completely and utterly frank, when you wrote *A Domestic Animal*.

'Yes, that was the first time I came absolutely clean and was totally frank. It was very interesting when that book appeared. I think that it is one of my better books – not my best, but one of the better ones – yet some of the reviewers were very grudging. I'm absolutely convinced that they were people who wished to appear tolerant, and therefore they couldn't say, "This book disgusts us," so they found fault with it on a literary level. What I think they really disliked was the theme and the frankness of the theme.

'Of course, since it appeared the climate of opinion has changed, so when it was reissued in paperback the reviews were much more favourable.

'Of all my books it's the one that is closest to my own experience, the one that betrayed the most of myself. One of the criticisms that's sometimes made of my work is that I'm too detached from my people, and this is a book in which I was completely involved. But the same critics who would say, "He's too detached; he takes this Olympian view of his characters," were then critical because I seemed to be self-indulgent by identifying myself too closely with my characters. I think it is certainly true that if a heterosexual writes a book which is self-confessional of that kind, he is not going to be criticised in the same way.'

Was it an easy book to write?

'It wrote itself very easily. The extraordinary thing is that normally, when I experience things, I find they have to be reshaped and transformed to give artistic unity and shape. With *A Domestic Animal* the actual experience had an artistic unity. So it was very close to autobiography. Obviously for reasons of libel it couldn't be a complete autobiography, but all the events were based on things that really happened. There was very little invention in it.

'I wrote it very, very rapidly – it came very quickly indeed. I usually have tremendous doubts about my work, and when a book is finished I wonder whether it is quite good enough. But I never had any doubts about that book at all, so I was slightly disappointed by its reception.'

You once said that after writing *A Domestic Animal* you had 'exorcised' your desire to write again about a homosexual relationship.

'Well, for the moment, yes. I daresay I might feel the desire again. I'd never written exactly as I'd wanted to because of the difficulty of being totally explicit. At the period when I wrote *The Man On The Rock* it was impossible to be totally frank. Longmans, who were my publishers at the time, were rather stuffy anyway, so I made it that the American was obviously in love with the Greek boy, but in fact they never go to bed together. I think this is a sort of falsification. If I wrote that book now they would certainly have gone to bed. That's how I thought of it and I fudged it there, and to that extent the book isn't as good as it should be.'

What attracted you to the theme of paedophilia in *The Needle*?

'I don't know why. I'm not in fact a paedophile – if anything I'm the reverse. I'm not very interested in children. I don't particularly like them. I get on well with certain children but I'm not a person who's naturally a child-lover, so I don't know what particularly attracted me to that.

'What interested me far more was the brother/sister relationship, and I wanted some sort of guilty secret. And I thought, well, homosexuality now is not sufficiently terrible in the eyes of the world at large for it to be a guilty secret. So I wanted something rather "worse" as the world would see it. I think that's what really attracted me.

'It's still a taboo which I don't think homosexuality is any longer. I think paedophilia is, and incest is, and death. These are the three remaining taboos. And cannibalism I suppose.'

74

One aspect of your writing, particularly in the early novels, is a concern about the privacy of individuals. A great deal of conflict arises out of one character trespassing on the privacy of another. How unhappy a view of human relationships is that?

'I think for many years I did have this deeply pessimistic view of human relationships. But my life has changed enormously, in so far as in Japan I had a very satisfactory relationship with another person which I had never had before. And I have a very satisfactory relationship now. So now I do see that it is possible to have a very happy relationship. Previously they'd all been very transitory or totally unsatisfactory. This has obviously changed my view and I have a less pessimistic view now. I used to think that there was always one person who kisses and one who offers his cheek; one person who was hunted and one person who was hunting. The idea of reciprocity seemed to me very difficult – but I now think of it as something that is possible, and something which happens more frequently in life than I had imagined then.'

Your earlier pessimistic view sounds rather like that of your friend Joe Ackerley.

'Yes. He was a person who never found a reciprocal relationship. And he would frustrate himself to the extent that if somebody returned his love this somehow put him off. He wanted to be the person who was hunting the unobtainable. When the unobtainable became obtainable then he ceased to be desirable. And I think I was rather in that position myself for many years. Ackerley was always looking for the Ideal Friend and I would say to him, look, the Ideal Friend doesn't exist. You've got to make a compromise. It was something I realised when I was forty-five, or a little earlier, that you could never obtain a person who is exactly as you would desire him in fantasy. I think Ackerley never learned that.'

Were you anxious about Joe Ackerley's letters to you being published in the Braybrooke edition of his correspondence?

'No, no. He (Braybrooke) asked me if I minded what was published and I said, no, I didn't mind at all.

'There were one or two disobliging remarks about me in the letters – as happens in any friendship. Moments of irritation when you write something critical about a friend when you're annoyed with him. I didn't mind that either.

'I remember when Joe was staying with me in Kyoto he wrote to other people that he was thinking of staying with James Kirkup in Sendai because he didn't like the over-busy sort of life – as he saw it – rushing around and going to gay bars. But when he was with James Kirkup in Sendai then he was longing to be back in Kyoto in what he saw as the greater comfort of my house. This I didn't mind at all because it's perfectly human, and everyone does that sort of thing.

'But what was very funny about Ackerley's stay in Kyoto was that in fact I was not a person who went to an enormous number of gay bars. But I thought that as Ackerley was a visitor I should take him. So after a very tiring day when I wanted to stay at home, I used to think I must take him around the gay bars. And then I saw his letters, and very often he would be thinking, "Oh God, why am I being dragged around these gay bars? I don't want to do it."

'So each thought the other wanted it.'

Joe Ackerley published your poetry in *The Listener*.

'Yes. He was the first literary editor who encouraged me a great deal. But he was strange, because at first he was not at all eager that we should meet. I mean, he'd published my poetry for quite a long time, and he used to write me letters about my work when I was working on the land – I even used to review novels for *The Listener* and he used to send me them by post. He'd write comments on my reviews without, however, our ever meeting.

'Then finally we met and slowly became good friends. But there was another strange thing about him – he didn't like his friends to meet one another. Now I was very eager to meet E.M. Forster because I had an enormous admiration for him and Joe Ackerley was his closest friend at that period. I'd heard from some other people that Forster wanted to meet me, so I asked Ackerley to let me meet him. But it was years and years before he brought us together.

76

'I don't know what the reason was. If I have two friends who I think will get on, my first impulse is to bring them together. Ackerley would always keep them apart. William Plomer was another person – I never met him through Joe. When I did meet him it was at a literary party. I admired his poetry and I used to say to Joe Ackerley how much I'd like to meet William Plomer, and he'd reply, well he's rather a recluse and he doesn't really like meeting people. But I think he just didn't care for people to get together. Whether it was that he was frightened they would talk about him and somehow compare notes, or whether he had a kind of possessiveness about people I don't know.'

When you eventually met Morgan Forster you weren't overly impressed.

'I was impressed by him, but I felt there was something old-maidish and finicky about him. One thing that put me off him very much was when Joe Ackerley told me that Forster would allow his friends a certain amount of latitude and then if they did something that offended him they were cast into outer darkness and he would never speak to them again.

'There were certain people who, as it were, had "grace" and others who hadn't. I couldn't understand that. I feel that if people offend you they must be able to work their passage back, and similarly if you yourself offend a friend, you have a row, then you hope that by being pleasant to him later, or by doing him a good turn, that the friendship can be renewed. Everyone at some point falls below the standard you set, but apparently Forster would decide that someone had fallen below the standard *he* set and that was the end of that particular person.

'I found this rather unattractive – it put me off him. And I did feel that there was this sort of slightly coy, feline, old-maidish side to him which I found unappealing. But I didn't get to know Forster well and I'm probably misjudging him.'

We haven't talked about influences much. You have in the past acknowledged influences on your work. Which were the main ones?

'When I worked on the land I read enormously. Isher-wood for instance – I don't think I've ever mentioned his

77

influence before – he was a person who influenced me very much. It's very difficult for people nowadays to realise how important we all regarded Isherwood. We felt he was going to be the major novelist of his time. He had this enormous influence on writers of my generation. We all read *Mr Norris Changes Trains*, *The Memorial* and so on. We felt here is a potentially major novelist; and although he's still a very good novelist he just never fulfilled that expectation.

'Then Somerset Maugham has this great influence from the point of view of technique, his narrative technique, from which I think his nephew Robin has obviously learned a great deal. The ability to tell a story so that the readers are actually carried along is something I like to think that I've also got.

'I find this with Robin Maugham's work – once I start on a Robin Maugham novel, there are things I may not like in it but I've got to push on – and this is simply a mastery of technique.

'Proust was another influence, and Forster had an influence – but more on the view I took of the world rather than on how I wrote.

'And then a novelist who had an influence on me, but is now very little read, was Forrest Reid. It's not an influence that has persisted, but it was very much there in my book *Never Again* – the style, the way it was written, the lucidity of style.

'It was not until I wrote *The Dividing Stream* that I felt I had a voice of my own. When I was re-reading *To The Dark Tower* I would pick up echoes of other writers, Isherwood, Henry Green, other writers who'd interested me. And it isn't until that fourth book that I suddenly feel I've acquired, as every writer eventually must, a voice of my own. It wan't an echo of Maugham's voice or Forster's voice.'

How closely were you involved with L.P. Hartley? You worked on his book *Poor Claire*.

'Yes, I knew him well, but at the end of his life. He was a great friend of a great friend of mine called Clifford Kitchen, whom I knew far better and whose work I admired very much. He's not a particularly well-known writer but I think he was perhaps a better writer than Hartley. He didn't have that same charm which Hartley had and which won him a big readership. So Kitchen never had the same sort of success.

'I met Hartley through Clifford Kitchen, and I used to go and see them. Both of them were very frightened of the modern world and I see now that my value to them, I think, was that I brought them news of the world. They would question me about the sort of life I was leading. They would ask me about the gay bars in Brighton, or gay bars in London, and clubs and so on. They would never dream of going to one themselves. They wanted to hear all about it, though.

'They lived rather like recluses and I think this was the value I had for both of them near the end of their lives.

'Kitchen was the exact opposite of Hartley because he had a very abrasive exterior. People often used to say he was a difficult man, rather chilly and unfriendly. In fact he was warm-hearted and kind; whereas Hartley, underneath all the teddy-bear charm, had a streak of ruthlessness and a tremendous sense of self-preservation.

'He would never come clean about being homosexual. To me, of course, he was totally frank, but since his death I've met a lot of his friends who were absolutely amazed that he should have been gay.

'He was very, very frightened of coming out. Of course as he grew older he became less and less discreet in his novels – but he was nervous about some of those later novels. He used to say "What will Lady So-and-So say when she reads this?" And I thought, hell, what does it matter? In any case nowadays nobody's going to be particularly upset. But after some of those later novels, *My Brother's Keeper* for example, he was worried what his grand friends were going to say about it.

'I worked on *Poor Claire* with him because he'd got into a total muddle. He had piles of manuscripts – I think there were about five different versions. So all this was sent to me, and he said, "Do what you can with it."

'I had no idea what he was trying to do, so I rang him up and said can you give me some idea. And he said, "I'm not really sure." It was very difficult. I decided what the basic theme was – putting people under obligations by giving them gifts, and by giving them gifts in a way you estrange them – and this is what I tried to bring out from the muddle of chapters, many of which were in three, four or five drafts.

'I don't think it was one of his best books.'

Are you working on a novel yourself at the moment?

'Not at the moment, no. I've just completed a book of short stories which I've handed to my publisher. But I have in fact got a novel which has been completed which will come out the following year. I've got to rewrite it, but it's been completed in its first draft. So I'm going to work on that in the autumn. The Rockerfeller Foundation have what they call a study centre on Lake Como. They've invited me to go there for a month and work on this revision. So that will be quite pleasant.'

You've done a good deal of travelling in your lifetime, but you've never visited the United States. You said once that the idea of America frightened you.

'Three times I've had the opportunity to go and each time I've somehow funked it and not been. Twice I've had invitations to universities there and once to a university in Canada, and on all those occasions at the last moment I've found, as I realise now, some excuse for not going. I had an invitation to go and teach in Dallas, just at the time of the Kennedy assassination, and told myself I don't want to go after this event. But I think now that this was a rationalisation and that I was really rather nervous about going to the States.

'I don't know why this should be because I've travelled to most other parts of the world. I know the Far East, I know all Europe, I know most of the Iron Curtain countries, but I've never been to America. I don't know why it should be – I just feel nervous about it. But I must some time take the plunge.'

Larry Kramer

There is almost a decade between the publication of Larry Kramer's highly controversial and sometimes reviled novel, *Faggots*, and the staging of his equally contentious AIDS play, *The Normal Heart* (which recently closed in London after a successful run of six months and sales of the text well in excess of ten thousand copies.) Over the course of those years things have changed . . .

'I now view *Faggots* as a historical novel,' states Kramer, an intense, articulate and cuddly New Yorker. 'It's like reading *Gone With the Wind*. It does seem a long time ago. But maybe people will be able to laugh at it more easily now. When I wrote it it was meant to be funny . . . '

Faggots is a long, picaresque novel – the action of which takes place over the course of a weekend – set in the gay sexual playground of New York. A kind of latter-day *Satyricon*, the book focuses on Fred Leamish, four days short of his fortieth birthday, who undertakes a voyage of (self) discovery into the world he inhabits ('This Faggot World.') Fred's voyage of discovery 'takes him into a world of saunas, baths, parties, discos, bars and clubs, private homes and public cruising areas,' I wrote in 1980, when reviewing the first British edition of *Faggots* for *The Literary Review*. But Fred does not find love – merely the sexual equivalent of junk food. He feels a sense of disgust which appears to have so annoyed the American activists – those who equate sex with sexual liberation.

'I was surprised by the hostile response to the book,' admits Kramer, reflecting back to the initial reaction to *Faggots*. 'You never get used to bad reviews, though as you get older you get *more* used to them. I was upset by a lot of the American gay community's reactions to the book. I've always been able to deal with self-criticism myself. It hurt, yeah, it hurt a lot – but those reactions strengthened me a lot. It was a good lesson to learn. And I had a lot of response from readers – three thousand letters, all positive. Not one nasty letter. *That's* where I learned . . . '

There is a very direct relationship between *Faggots* and *The Normal Heart*. The latter is very much a sequel to the former – the warning voice of the novel can be viewed retrospectively as prophetic.

'The gay political platform – especially in the U.S.A. – was promulgated by a very few people who did *not* speak for the people. They were sounding off, but they were only expressing *their* point of view. Until very recently their message was "promiscuity is all." They did not speak for the mass of people. But when I wrote *Faggots*, I didn't think that what I was screaming about was going to lead to death . . . '

But why was there such a delay between the novel and the play?

'I'm not a slow writer, but I write from my life,' says Kramer, 'so I had to take time to live the next chapter. Both *Faggots* and *The Normal Heart* are obviously autobiographical and, of course, I got caught up in the AIDS thing very early on. I realised that this was the thing I had to write about; it was incumbent on me to write about it. AIDS made me much more conscious of time, made me feel I'd got to write faster, to get out what's in me. *The Normal Heart* has given me an awful lot of confidence. It has been a success and the support from important people gives me confidence. That's been very important for me. Once started, I'm fast. It's getting started that takes a long time.'

There has still been remarkably little AIDS literature ('I worry about so many works out there about transvestites,' says Kramer, '*Torch Song Trilogy*, *Kiss of the Spiderwoman*, *La Cage aux Folles* . . . ') and Kramer's slightly hectoring stance has not enhanced his popularity with politically active gays in New York. Nor has it helped his relationships with other writers.

'I feel very much alone, I feel very isolated from my fellow gay activists,' he announces without bitterness but obviously with regret. 'I stood alone, I still do. Andrew Holleran, a close friend, still writes about the physical side of our lives. Ed White, another close friend, disagrees with me totally – politically. I guess I'm considered a pariah . . . '

It will be interesting to see what response *Faggots* elicits from British critics the second time around; the success of *The Normal Heart* should at least provoke the interest that was notably absent when Futura published the book in 1980. I still think it one of the major gay novels to have appeared from that first full-bodied American flowering of gay literature in the mid-to-late seventies and I can do no better than once again to quote from my original review: 'Mr Kramer's view is a personal one – and it must always be remembered that anyone's perceptions are distorted through the prism of their own beliefs, ideals and desires. Because *Faggots* is so obviously a personal narrative, written out of real conviction, it should not be condemned or dismissed. Activists may squeal at the portrait of homosexual living that Mr Kramer has drawn; puritans may faint clean away in horror or disgust. Those who read *Faggots* with due care and attention will discover a novel of deep and abiding morality; bitter, harshly humorous, grotesque, frightening, comic, and as honest as one individual's perceptions can make it.'

Hanif Kureishi

'I was born in London of an English mother and a Pakistani father,' Hanif Kureishi wrote in his essay, *The Rainbow Sign*, published in the same volume as his screenplay for *My Beautiful Laundrette* (1986). 'My father, who lives in London, came to England from Bombay in 1947 to be educated by the old colonial power. He married here and never went back to India. The rest of his large family, his brothers, their wives, his sisters, moved from Bombay to Karachi, in Pakistan, after partition.'

In that simple declarative paragraph, Kureishi lays out most of the essentials of the plot of his first novel.

The Buddha of Suburbia is a rich, picaresque novel which – because of its multi-layered plot and diversity of characters who occasionally border on the outlandish – has a flavour that could be described as Dickensian. The novel is a growing-up and coming-to-terms portrait of Karim (half English, half Pakistani) as he progresses through callow youth in suburbia in the sixties to growing maturity as the Thatcher decade dawns.

Sexually adventurous, Karim is obsessed by the beautiful but manipulative Charlie (son of his father's stylish mistress Eva) and has had an on-going but essentially exploratory sexual relationship with his cousin Jamila for some years. Blossoming sexuality has to be explored; questions of race and identity have to be resolved. That Kureishi handles his delicate and complex themes with such consummate skill – and ribald humour – makes this a most auspicious debut.

We met in Hanif Kureishi's flat in West London – which I took to be the original of the apartment Karim, his

84

father and Eva move into in the novel. But it isn't. 'That was sold,' Kureishi told me. We sat in a spartan drawing room overlooking a central square. One wall was bare except for framed pictures lined up along the skirting-board. Two walls were covered floor-to-ceiling with books – everything from William L. Shirer's massive *The Rise and Fall of the Third Reich* to biographies of Ronald Firbank, Somerset Maugham and Richard Burton and novels ranging from Milan Kundera to Muriel Spark. Except for two dust jackets for *The Buddha of Suburbia*, there were no signs of his writing career – no reminders of his version of Brecht's *Mother Courage* at the National Theatre, no posters for *My Beautiful Laundrette* or *Sammy and Rosie Get Laid*.

In his essay *The Rainbow Sign*, Kureishi has written that *My Beautiful Laundrette* started life as an epic, tracing a family from the Indian sub-continent to Britain and their life thereafter. Is *The Buddha of Suburbia* a more concerted effort to get to grips with that same material?

'I suppose it is, really,' Kureishi agreed. 'It was very difficult to get all that into a film, especially a British film because they are so small-scale. I couldn't be too ambitious, especially as *Laundrette* was my first film. When the novel was finished, the story of a family was still not told. I'd always wanted to start off with an epic, although the novel is *not* an epic. But you can still get more into a book than you can get into a film.'

In that already mentioned essay, Kureishi intimates that *Laundrette* is autobiographical. As *Buddha* charts much of the same territory, can it be assumed that it too is autobiographical?

'The novel is less autobiographical than you might think,' he corrected. 'The atmosphere *is* autobiographical. Like Karim, I grew up in Bromley in Kent and the suburbs. But unlike Karim, I was never an actor and my father never ran away with a woman like Eva. The book is *emotionally* autobiographical, rather than being based on events that happened as described.'

Though the novel is set during a recognisable historical

85

period – the boundaries are basically musical – the transition from the hippie sixties to the punk late seventies is handled in such a way as to make the boundaries appear contiguous. Was this a deliberate attempt at reinventing the historical time-scale?

'I found the time thing very difficult to do. It was partly to do with what happened in the music. We were listening to Pink Floyd, Barclay James Harvest and David Bowie. Then when punk came along it swept it all away. It seemed to be another era. But you must remember we were still having the sixties in Bromley in 1974. When Helen talks about running away to San Francisco, everything she'd have liked about it was well over by then.' He paused for a moment. 'I was back in Bromley only the other day . . . people there have just started wearing their hair in mohicans . . .'

There is a far more concrete expression about overt racism in the *The Rainbow Sign* than appears in either *Laundrette* or *Buddha* – was this because it was easier to write about implicitly in the novel or because the subject belonged more in an essay?

'It was partly to do with the feeling that I'd dealt with it in *The Rainbow Sign* and didn't want to go over all that again. But I also felt that the whole novel was about what it's like to be a black or Asian person in Britain. There's no one in the book that Karim deals with who *doesn't* take his racial background into consideration. It's a part of the book rather than specific incidents.

'It does come more to the fore in the second half of the book – when Karim becomes an actor and has to black up to play Mowgli in *The Jungle Book* or play an illegal immigrant everyone laughs at. He seen as an actor who has to play parts like that. It's not overt racism, but to do with the way people see black and Asian people. But that said, there are specific incidents – Helen's father setting the dog on Karim, for instance . . .'

In both *Laundrette* and *Buddha* the gay (Johnny and Omar in the former) or bisexual (Karim and Charlie in the latter) characters don't seem to have any problems with prejudice specifically because of their sexuality . . .

'In *Laundrette*, I wanted their sexuality to be a virtue: I didn't want to make it a big deal. It just seemed right, perfectly natural that they were gay. Those blokes were gay just as other people were straight.

'In *Buddha*, the bisexuality has more to do with growing up in the late sixties – when there wasn't any sexual morality. You discovered your sexuality by messing around, seeing what you liked. There seemed to be a lot of gay people around then and even though places like Bromley were very prim, you didn't feel any pressure because everyone lived so privately. Karim's sexuality does not have any morality attached. At the beginning of the book he doesn't really have *any* values. He does what gives him pleasure. He doesn't see other people as objects of concern . . . '

'Received a letter from an aunt who lives in the north of England. After seeing *Laundrette* she frequently rings my father to abuse him,' Kureishi wrote in *Some Time With Stephen: A Diary*, published in the same volume as the screenplay for *Sammy and Rosie Get Laid* (1988). ' "Your son is a complete bastard!" she screeches down the phone, as if it's my father's fault I write such things. "Can't you control the little bastard!" she yells. "Humiliating us in public! Suppose people find out I'm related to him!" Is Kureishi expecting similar responses from his family once they read *The Buddha of Suburbia*?

'Probably. But my mum likes *Laundrette* now. She didn't when it first came out. She sensibly hasn't read the novel; she knows there's "filth" on every page. But relatives don't mind if you're a "dirty boy" but successful. If you've got your book published you're all right.

'But part of the Asian community is very hostile about work like mine and, of course, much more so about work by Salman Rushdie. When *Laundrette* opened in New York, there were demonstrations against it. I used to walk up and down with the pickets, not saying who I was. "Why don't you like this film?" I'd ask. "Because Hanif Kureishi says all Pakistani men are homosexual," they'd say . . . '

We talked about the problems of positive imaging –

'Usually people who want positive images don't know anything about writing,' Kureishi stated. 'Asking for positive images is asking for characters who are less than human. If you had to provide positive images all the time, you wouldn't be able to draw anyone who was fully rounded . . . '

Hanif Kureishi has been a great supporter of his friend Salman Rushdie throughout *The Satanic Verses* affair. He, too, has been pretty equivocal about Islam . . .

'But I don't think I've said anything that would inspire anyone to run out and buy a box of matches to burn *Buddha*. It's a shame that that's what's happened to Rushdie. If you can't write what you want to write about this person or that person, you'd be all the time thinking about what you could write. It's a bit like people who don't like having their photograph taken because of their fear that the photograph will steal their souls. In a way Muslims protesting about *The Satanic Verses* have further marginalised themselves in British society because of their fear of being portrayed as anyone else would be. And you do have to take sides: people who are Muslim or have Muslim names say, "Hey, that's not me . . . " For example, there are many left-wing Muslims who aren't going to have anything to do with these people. I'm not on the right, I'm not a Muslim fundamentalist. I believe all writers should be able to write about what they want. I don't think any group can ask for special privileges – but the price of free speech is that you may be vilified and abused.'

With his first novel behind him – and translation rights in thirteen languages pre-sold before British publication – what will Kureishi be concentrating on in the future: plays, films or fiction?

'Writing novels was always the thing I wanted to do most. When I was fourteen the thing I really wanted to write was novels. Those got waylaid by plays and films. Then after *Laundrette* and *Sammy and Rosie* I had the money, for the first time in my life, to buy the time to write a novel. In film the camera can describe a scene; in fiction you have to do that yourself . . . Writing the novel partly came out of the feeling that *Sammy and Rosie* was a bit crowded as a film, a feeling that I needed a medium in which I didn't have to crowd so much in. Plays and films are all cutting back, but in a novel you really feel you can spread out. In fact, I don't think I'll write plays any more. I'll concentrate on films and another novel.'

Finally, in part, was writing *The Buddha of Suburbia* an act of resolution?

'It's true that there's a sense in which you have something on your mind to do with your past – race, sex, father – and when you sit down to write about it you have the time to explore it in depth. The thing most on my mind was to do with race. Being half Pakistani and half English. I think I've worked out what it means – because I've been writing about it for so long.

'But I wouldn't like to think that the writing was only about that. When you're writing, you do have to feel that you're communicating. I like to think I've written a pop book or a popular book, not an esoteric book for people who work in universities. I'd like to think that *The Buddha of Suburbia* is a book for young people to read in bed.'

Gavin Lambert

Gavin Lambert's best-known work is *Inside Daisy Clover*; the story of a Judy Garland-like child star and the problems she faces as she grows up. The book was published in 1963; the movie followed in 1965 (with a cast which included Natalie Wood as Daisy, Christopher Plummer, Ruth Gordon and Robert Redford).

A long time expatriate, Lambert lived for nearly fifteen years in Los Angeles and since 1973 has been resident in Tangiers. His body of work is small but impressive – a series of novels with Los Angeles/Hollywood locations: *The Slide Area*, *Inside Daisy Clover*, *A Case for the Angels*, *The Goodbye People*, *Norman's Letter*; two books on movies: *The Making of Gone With the Wind*, and *On Cukor*; and, most recently, his first London-based novel, *In the Night All Cats Are Grey*, a bleak and chilling novel about total isolation. Gavin Lambert's screenplays include *Sons and Lovers*, for which he received an Oscar nomination; *Inside Daisy Clover*; and *The Roman Spring of Mrs Stone* – which, in his *Memoirs*, Tennessee Williams describes as 'My favourite of all the movies based on my work.'

Recently in London to promote his new novel, we met and talked in the cramped office of his publisher's publicist.

'I started, really, as editor of *Sight and Sound* and also did a certain amount of freelance film criticism for about six years. Then I was offered a job in Hollywood by Nicholas Ray – a couple of years or so after he'd directed *Rebel Without A Cause*. He had a contract to make a couple of pictures at Twentieth-Century Fox and asked me to be his personal assistant. One that turned out quite interestingly was called *Bigger Than Life* with James Mason. It was marvellous experience. First of all, I went to Hollywood to a working situation and met lots of people. Then, as personal assistant, you really have to do a bit of everything – you are an ideas person; you're in on script conferences; you're on the set every day; you're in on the cutting and so on. It was a wonderful entrée into the whole movie world.'

Did you work very closely with Tennessee Williams on *The Roman Spring of Mrs Stone*?

'Not very closely, no. He gave me a very free hand. Of course, it was an entirely different project from the other Tennessee Williams films because it was a novel and not a play and therefore there was more work to be done. Most of the adaptations of Tennessee Williams's plays have been pretty straightforward. Just a question of cutting little scenes here and there. But the novel – which was a short novel – had to be expanded and it called for a certain amount of invention. Tennessee oversaw everything and had two or three very good ideas. But in the main I worked independently from him.'

I understand that you worked on a screenplay with Christopher Isherwood.

'Yes. Which was never done. It wasn't really a screenplay; it was a long treatment. It was a story he had written in collaboration with someone else – a man, I think, called Lester Samuels – seven years previously. It had never been sold. Isherwood showed it to me and I had some ideas about it. We did a second version, a longer version – and it was on the verge of being sold two or three times.'

It is obvious from your novels that you found Hollywood produced an awful lot of material.

'An infinite amount. It is an extraordinary place. I really date my career as a novelist from there – *The Slide Area* and *Inside Daisy Clover*.'

Was the character of Daisy Clover consciously based upon Judy Garland – whom she more than superficially resembles?

'Of course I thought of Judy Garland. You couldn't not think of her. But Daisy Clover is not so much based on Judy Garland as Judy Garland is an element in the character. Not so much the character as what happened to her. The idea of someone with that kind of extraordinary popular talent who was really quite a private person but had to adjust to being owned by everybody. That much was her. Although I had never met Judy Garland before I wrote the book, I met her later and was very pleased when I discovered she liked it.'

And then you wrote the screenplay for the film – were you happy with it?

'Fifty-fifty. There were things I liked about it and things I was disappointed with. I wanted it to be funnier. I think it was a bit lacking in humour; a little serious in the wrong way at times. On the other hand I thought it had a lot of style and atmosphere. And the acting I liked very much.'

In what must have been one of his first movies, Robert Redford played Daisy's gay husband – what was he like to work with and why was the character changed so much from the book?

'Redford was wonderful to work with. It was his first really important part. It was the most difficult part in the movie because it was the most ambiguous. Of course, it was ten years ago, that film. It's amazing how much it's opened up. But the homosexual thing was quite a problem then. Of course, in the book, he was simply a homosexual actor. But it was decided *that* was too much for the time. So I suggested that we make him a bisexual. That seemed to go down very well . . . but at the last moment – it was written quite openly as that – people got more and more scared. Cold feet were very evident when those scenes were going to be shot and they were trimmed – not by me – and they were finally trimmed so much that it was impossible to make out what was going on. We had to put lines back – not enough lines – because it was too vague on that issue. But that was simply the time and what people thought were the pressures. Alas, my word was not final.'

But surely *Inside Daisy Clover* came after one or two movies with a more or less explicit homosexual theme, *Suddenly Last Summer*, for example?

'Yes, but in *Suddenly Last Summer* Sebastian came to a bad end. Here, Wade Lewis didn't. This was the whole thing. As far as I was concerned there was no guilt involved – except when we made him a bisexual there was a certain amount of guilt written in because he married Daisy and led her up the garden path to some extent. But he didn't pay for it – *at all*! In fact, as a I originally wrote it, when Wade came back to see Daisy in the hospital towards the end of the movie, I wanted his friend with him. Just standing there in the background waiting – to show that Wade's life was going on.'

In *A Case For the Angels*, in which you take a look at – to use a rather outmoded word – the hippy life-style, you rather seem to disapprove. Do you disapprove of that particular way of life?

'I don't think disapproval is the word. It wasn't for me, I would say. I don't think approval or disapproval come into it. I accept it as a way other people were living at that time and I was sort of trying to present their justification or rationalisation or whatever you like to call it without comment – because I don't think that the protagonist of the novel is, for that matter, above reproach either. I was trying to show the life, weaknesses and problems of both sides. So I wasn't really for or against. I was just looking at it . . . '

With *The Slide Area*, *Inside Daisy Clover* and *A Case For the Angels* you seem to chart your charm and gradual disenchantment with that whole Los Angeles way of life.

'In the beginning it is enchantment, yes. There may be a beginning of disenchantment – but disenchantment is different from disapproval. I'm not prepared to say it's wrong. I simply didn't like it in the end. It's very strange there now – though I was there last year and to me it's still an absolutely fascinating place. But part of the fascination is from when I was there and liked it – it's hanging over. But it still does seem to me unlike any place in the world. It's like outer space. I find it depressing. This awful emptiness. This whole façade of sexuality and the lack of *real* sexuality there. People cannot just turn on to each other. There has to be a gimmick. There's got to be the dirty movie or the waterbed or the dancing or something. There is this absolute terror of two people just being with each other. New York is quite different. In New York it is still possible to have a one-to-one thing with people. In Los Angeles it's very different – they don't want it.'

Why did you leave Los Angeles and go to Tangiers?

'A combination of things . . . I'd been to Tangiers before several times; I'd been all over Morocco, in fact, and I'd always liked it very much – and, somehow, in the back of my mind, was the thought that if I got tired of Los Angeles, Tangiers might be the place. And increasingly there wasn't enough to keep me in L.A.'

Have you thought of doing a Tangerine novel?

'Not in the sense that most people do Tangerine novels – because I don't like them very much. Most people write Tangiers novels when they are about to leave Tangiers and they're somehow disgruntled with it and are having revenge upon it. I feel that the kind of revenge they take is rather petty. You can find a silly expatriate colony almost anywhere and I don't think they're very interesting to write about. There's also a lot of the pot calling the kettle black.'

In The Night All the Cats Are Grey came as rather a surprise to me. Yet I always look for connections and this novel seemed to be the furthest point you could go in a series of novels which have all been about isolation – in one way or another.

'I think so. I hope so.'

Was Simpson, the librarian whom the narrator works with, written as a gay character?

'Suppressed, I would say. I wanted to intimate that she had never faced it and that she lived with this other woman but doubted whether they'd ever got beyond petting. It's a very common thing. One often sees women of a certain age who have perhaps both been married and not particularly enjoyed it having a sort of companionship which could really go further. But they are not prepared to take it there. First of all, women in that kind of situation seem to turn off sex – and I think men don't. Or less of them, anyway.'

Do you think that you have a very pessimistic view of life?

'I don't know. I certainly haven't got a totally *optimistic* view of life. I suppose I'm pessimistic in the sense that though I don't think we're all going to destroy ourselves in thirty years, I do think that in thirty years' time life is going to be very difficult, very disagreeable. That, I feel strongly.'

I think my use of the word pessimistic was meant rather more personally. There seems to be a sense in your work that relationships are always going to be unequal. That there will always be the hunter and the hunted and that one person is going to suffer.

'That's true – as regards people getting together I'm not pessimistic about that – they still manage to; thank God. Just about successfully sometimes. But even if you only do it for a couple of years it's O.K. It's better than nothing. I've never done it for more than about four years. But that's all right too. The great thing is to try.'

John Lehmann

Born in 1907, John Lehmann grew up in a privileged atmosphere both comfortable and intelligent. One sister is actress Beatrix Lehmann (one of the most notable interpreters of Eugene O'Neill's plays); another sister is novelist Rosamond Lehmann. After an education at Eton and Cambridge, Lehmann moved into the world of publishing – he was closely involved with Leonard and Virginia Woolf (to whom he introduced the young Christopher Isherwood.) One of the younger members of the Bloomsbury Group, John Lehmann counted among his friends such notables as Lytton Strachey.

Though an inveterate traveller Lehmann didn't lose touch with publishing. Long periods spent in Vienna and Berlin, and travels about pre-Second World War Europe, enabled him to meet many of the writers, poets and painters he was later to publish in *New Writing* and *Penguin New Writing*. Almost immediately after the war Lehmann established his own publishing house – John Lehmann Ltd – which was first British publisher for several major American writers (Gore Vidal, Saul Bellow, Paul Bowles, Tennessee Williams.)

Distinguished as both publisher and poet, in recent years John Lehmann has published a fascinating three-volume memoir (now unfortunately out of print), poetry, and, most recently, *In The Purely Pagan Sense*, a novel which tells the story of a happy homosexual called Jack Marlowe (whose life bears a marked resemblance to that of the author.)

We interviewed Lehmann in his London flat, talking in a drawing room dominated by crowded bookshelves, a massive desk and picture-filled walls (Duncan Grant,

Denton Welch, Cecil Beaton, Keith Vaughan, John Piper.) The mantelpiece was cluttered with invitations; photographs of family and friends – William Plomer, Virginia Woolf, Christopher Isherwood; sisters Rosamond, Helen, and Beatrix; Edith Sitwell – were dotted about the room. Side-tables were piled high with books and magazines – everything from travel brochures to *The Virginia Woolf Quarterly*.

Can you tell us something about the Hogarth Press and the Woolfs?

'Yes, I certainly can. I have, of course, written about it in my autobiography but what was fascinating to me was that I'd always wanted to have something to do with publishing and here was a little firm where the personal touch was everything and they were keenly interested in new books and new authors and had a very high literary standard.'

With the Hogarth Press and later with *New Writing* there seems to have been an awareness of what today is called 'gay sensibility.'

'I think that's only partly true. It is true that just at that time – when I joined the Hogarth Press – I made friends with Stephen Spender who introduced me to Christopher Isherwood, and I was very excited by the novel which Christopher sent me, *The Memorial*, which had failed to get a publisher at that time. I immediately wanted to publish it and managed to persuade Leonard and Virgina Woolf to do so. And, of course, I've always been the keenest admirer of Christoper Isherwood ever since. He's made no bones about the fact that he is homosexual and I think one can say, now that he's dead, that Wystan Auden was homosexual too. William Plomer was undoubtedly homosexual; I think one can say that absolutely frankly. Of course *Sado* is a completely homosexual book. *Sado* was originally a much longer book and Leonard and Virginia managed to persuade William Plomer to cut it down because it got rather out of control. I often wonder what that book would have been like if William had written it in 1970 instead of 1930 or whenever it was.

'Christopher Isherwood, William Plomer, Joe Ackerley and E.M. Forster were all very close to one another. They formed a very happy quartet, if you like to put it that way. I began to know Forster in the thirties and I saw quite a lot of him during the war and afterwards. We became very good friends. I read *Maurice* in the early fifties. As a matter of fact, I was one of many people who read it. I think I agreed with most people who felt that it wasn't vintage Forster. And, of course, it's not. The version I read was not the version which was published; it was a previous version. I thought (a) that it might do his reputation some harm and (b) that if it were published during his lifetime it might seem rather out of date. I read it when books like Gore Vidal's *City and the Pillar* had appeared and a lot more was already appearing dealing fairly frankly with homosexual themes. I had a feeling, and I think this was shared by other people who had read *Maurice*, that the book would seem rather shy and old-fashioned. As a posthumous book it was very different, of course.'

Don't you think that even posthumous publication of *Maurice* did harm to Forster's reputation?

'I doubt it. There were some very good reviews indeed, including reviews in America. What I think may have harmed his reputation is the book of short pieces which came out later – *The Life to Come & Other Stories*. They were really very trivial. There were one or two good pieces, but apart from that it seemed almost doodling.'

Forster always worked very hard on his books, yet less effort seems to have gone into *Maurice*; do you think this was because he knew it wouldn't be published in his lifetime?

'I think that's quite possible. On the other hand I do feel that there's an element of fantasy in the sense of sort of wish-dreaming in it that's not characteristic of Forster's best books.'

The same kind of fantasising which D.H. Lawrence indulged in – most apparently in *Lady Chatterley's Lover*?

'Yes, I think there is a parallel.'

How well did you know Lytton Strachey?

'I knew him quite well for a limited number of years, because, as you must remember, he died early. I got to know him during my Cambridge days and then saw quite a bit of him soon after. He was a most delightful person to know – enormously kind to young men he thought would appreciate what he liked and looked for.'

In your new novel, *In The Purely Pagan Sense*, the hero, Jack Marlowe, is seduced by a character called Babbington who bears a marked resemblance to Strachey. As points in Marlowe's life seem to coincide with points in your own life can we ask if you were seduced by Lytton Strachey?

'Jack Marlowe's experience sometimes comes close to my own . . .'

It seems probable that a number of your readers and certainly some of your reviewers will read *In The Purely Pagan Sense* as a supplement to your autobiography. It certainly seems to fill in the personal side of your life.

'I expected that. At the same time I absolutely see your point, but I do want to stress that this is fiction. The people are imaginary. I did start off with the idea of writing the novel as autobiography – it was some years ago – but as soon as I got my teeth into it, I realised it wouldn't do. Too boring, for one thing, but mainly there were too many living people involved. So I turned it into a fictional confession, making composite characters and changing times and places and so on. One instance; Jack Marlowe has a younger brother, but I have not got a brother.'

How did you view *In The Purely Pagan Sense*? Is it a statement from you?

'Yes, I suppose in a certain sense it is. I think it's a statement about what life was like for a homosexual during my lifetime. From that point of view, I think I've tried to restrain fantasy very much. I mean, there are the obvious fantasy bits in it but they are deliberate fantasy things and they have nothing to do with the action of the book. I would say that everything that takes place in the book – in the sense of any homosexual episode – is factually true.'

Could one take the novel as a 'coming out' statement?

'You mean saying "I am a homosexual"? Well, in a certain sense, it is, isn't it? But that doesn't mean that it follows my life or anything like that. With that reservation, I would agree with you.'

Your book is a very happy book yet obviously the times in which it is set were difficult if one were homosexual.

'It was very difficult. But if one had friends who were homosexual and who moved in a world which accepted homosexuals – which was certainly true in the Bloomsbury Group – there was no feeling of hostility or prejudice, whether they were lesbians or male homosexuals. In a sense I was lucky to have been brought up in the atmosphere in which, for instance, Leonard and Virginia Woolf didn't care tuppence whether one loved one's sex or not.'

Presumably the same situation existed with Ottoline Morrell?

'Yes, of course. I must say as fond as I was of the Bloomsbury Group and particularly fond of Virginia Woolf and E.M. Forster and Lytton Strachey, I do think they behaved abominably to Ottoline. Really quite abominably. As someone said recently, it wasn't merely a question of biting the hand that fed you, it was chopping it off at the shoulder. She was an awfully kind person, Ottoline, you know. She wasn't brilliant in any way – what she had was a gift for knowing perhaps instinctively whether someone was a good writer or a good painter. She knew. Perhaps she couldn't explain her feelings, but she knew, and she'd tolerate anything.'

Homosexual society is very classless because you can work up or stay working-class or whatever. It seems far easier to move up and down with facility.

'Jack Marlowe says in the book that the point about homosexual relations in society is that they move vertically through all classes. And it's always been so. It always will be so as long as class exists. Which will probably last in this country longer than anywhere else.

'I think homosexual boys, whatever their class, have to break away from their parents very much. It's very sad. And I think that acceptance at the parental level is easier – has been easier – in educated and sophisticated circles. That is true. But as a corollary to that, I would like to say that when I began to get to know the homosexual world, particularly in the war and after – I'm not speaking about the homosexual *world*, but in this country – I was very much struck by the fact that just as many homosexuals came from the working class, or what you might like to call the lower middle class, as from the upper levels of society. In Russia, before the Revolution, they used to call homosexuality "officers' games" which indicated the point of view of homosexuality as a rich man's vice. Of course you must also remember, in relation to that, that highly educated levels of society probably read a lot of books in which it's treated. The classics which up until fifty years ago every young man who went to a public school and to university was brought up on were absolutely riddled with homosexuality.'

One of the experiences Jack Marlowe has is the beating one . . .

'Now what do you think the attitude of the reviewers or the public will be about the flagellation part of the novel?'

It's very honest, very refreshing, particularly at the moment as there's a lot of interest in that kind of thing.

'The whole psychology of sado-masochism.'

For homosexuals reading the book it's an especially interesting time to be reading of the experiences . . .

'I'm glad you think that because what I wanted to show was that one could have a sado-masochistic relationship with a young man yet be very loving towards him. That there could be a very real love relationship between two people involved in this purely sexual activity. That's rather what I wanted to indicate by that. And I'm sure it happens a great deal. My feeling is that it's spread much further than people admit or know.'

You obviously know about the gay organisations that exist – like the Campaign for Homosexual Equality, which was formed after the 1967 Sexual Offences Act . . .

'I don't know a great deal about them. I follow them as far as I can with interest. I've always felt that considering the amount of puritan prejudice there is in this country we were lucky to get the Act through. But as for the future I entirely agree that if young men are thought to be adults at the age of eighteen, and therefore responsible people who can make their own decisions, I cannot see why they shouldn't be thought responsible in choosing their sex partners. There seems to be a ludicrous anomaly there. But when you come to talking about people of sixteen or seventeen, I'm not quite so sure.'

But if for heterosexuals it's sixteen, it's difficult to accept the argument that it should be any different.

'I do see the force of that argument. What I'm really trying to say is there's no argument that will stand up to refusing to allow young men or women who have reached the age of eighteen not to choose their own sex partners. I don't think there's any argument at all that can stand up to it. When you come to people who are not of age in the technical sense, then I can see that there are slightly more difficulties. I won't say I'm not in sympathy with you, particularly as one knows that young boys are nearly always the seducers of older people. *Nearly* always. But I see absolutely no reason why young men of eighteen shouldn't be free to choose their sex partners. It seems ridiculous.

'I think people are either homosexuals – I mean I think something has happened by the time they're even seven or eight – and they will be either homosexual or heterosexual. And whatever happens to them at school – they make experiments at school, or they may make experiments when they are undergraduates at university – but they will turn back to their basic heterosexuality or homosexuality. I have no doubt about that. I think the idea of the corruption of people into becoming homosexuals is nonsense.'

The protection we need to have, and this applies to heterosexuals as well as homosexuals, is protection against exploitation, as I'm sure you've seen in your lifetime and one sees nowadays.

'But then, you see, I've seen a lot of boys in foreign countries – perhaps in this country too – who have decided that it's a good thing, that it will be useful to them to prostitute themselves – as homosexuals or for homosexuals. But I'm quite certain that many of those boys were not homosexuals and didn't become homosexuals by doing this. Bisexuals perhaps – I rather doubt whether they could have been successful on the game if they hadn't been bisexual at least.'

Brian Masters

'Overwhelmingly, what I want the reader of the book to feel is that he, the reader, is not unlike Nilsen himself. Not that we're all potential murderers, though I suppose we are; we're all capable of it. In one letter he wrote to me, Nilsen said, "Nobody is prepared to believe that I'm an ordinary man who has come to an overwhelming and extraordinary conclusion." If there is a theme to this book it's that I *do* believe he's an ordinary man who has come to that conclusion and that, therefore, it is perfectly possible for other ordinary men to descend into that kind of catastrophe given the right, or rather, the wrong, set of adverse influences working on him. We all have had bad influences working on us at some time or another – though we're usually strong enough to resist them.'

When Dennis Nilsen, a civil servant of Scottish origins, was arrested in connection with the discovery of human remains in a manhole outside his North London home, one of the most extraordinary murder cases in British history was about to explode into the nation's headlines. Within the next few days Nilsen confessed to a total of fifteen murders which he committed over a period of four years, the largest number attributed to a British killer.

Several aspects of the case – including his dismemberment of the corpses, his homosexuality and his necrophilia – ensured Nilsen enduring notoriety and the case the kind of sensational coverage that would keep newspaper readers titillated for months to come. Two books about the case appeared in the bookshops within days of the conclusion of Nilsen's trial – at which he was found guilty, sentenced to life imprisonment, and led to the cells with

103

the judge's recommendation that he serve no less than twenty-five years in prison.

Among those fascinated by the case was historical biographer Brian Masters – best known for his lives of popular novelist Marie Corelli and of Georgina, Duchess of Devonshire.

'When he was arrested I, like everyone else, saw the thing reported and thought, "There's more here than meets the eye. It looks like a very interesting case",' Masters told me when we met in the offices of the publishers of his book about Nilsen. 'I was struck by the fact there was a photograph of him being led out of the magistrates' court clutching a book under his arm, a complete works of Shakespeare. The juxtaposition of a man who was alleged to have cut people up and boiled their heads and was reading Shakespeare was so peculiar my curiosity was aroused.

'I'd never written a book about a criminal case and I thought it would be a very interesting thing to try and do. But first of all, I didn't think I'd be allowed; I thought there'd be obstacles put in my way; secondly, I thought that as the country's full of writers who are used to doing this kind of work, they'd be ahead of me.

'But I did one thing that nobody else thought of doing. I wasn't cunning; I was simply innocent. I wrote to Nilsen saying I was interested in his case and would like to write a book about it. But I told him I wouldn't do so without his consent. Had he said no, then I wouldn't have done it. There is no point in writing a book like this if it's just a stitching together of newspaper reports. The whole point in doing the book is to try to understand the man.

'While the Fleet Street boys were running all over the country interviewing anybody who'd ever stood next to Nilsen at a bus stop, nobody thought of writing to him. After my letter, he wrote me a letter which said, "Dear Mr Masters, I pass the burden of my life onto your shoulders," and asked me to go and see him. I was cleared by the Home Office and the relationship continued from then on. Throughout the eight months of his remand he was writing me a four-page letter every day; I saw him once a week – except towards the end: in the three or four weeks before the trial I used to visit him three times a week because he was getting very edgy then. He obviously wanted some kind of support; grew to rely on me. He's never said, "You will go on visiting me, won't you?" and I've never said that I would; but it's tacitly assumed that I will continue to visit him without either of us saying so.'

Had the mind of a murderer interested Masters before the Nilsen case?

'I've always been fascinated by the subject of murder and what produces that kind of breakdown, because one must recognise that murder is a sign of breakdown. In a sense the murderer is a victim as well. I'd always been interested but I'd never studied it and I'd also – like everyone – thought of a mu derer as a man who commits murder and that's all. I'd never bothered to think that there were other aspects of his life. So I've learned a great deal from writing this book; because there's a lot more to Nilsen than killing people. After all, it wasn't a full-time job. It is fascinating now for me to realise that a murderer is only an extreme instance of you and me. He's not a monster apart. He's a monster – but a monster with us, not apart from us.'

Since murders and murderers like Nilsen get an enormous amount of press coverage, does Masters think that the media and the public tend to treat them as entertainment?

'The general public view murder as entertainment, I think. The media, some parts of it, see murder simply as headlines. They're only interested in headlines; they're not interested in delving into reasons and motives and conclusions. It's very meretricious, their approach. Facile and frivolous; I wanted to do a serious study of the man and the influences in his life which produced this awful outcome. Because the book is not dramatic the drama is the greater. Writing about his origins, his life in the army, the civil service – there are clues on the way that some catastrophe is about to occur . . . but when it hits you at the beginning of chapter six it should knock you sideways . . .'

Killing for Company – the title originates from Nilsen's claim that his sense of isolation was a motivating cause of his murders; the victims of which quite literally became the companions to whom he returned after work – is a non-judgemental book, coolly dispassionate, and the more chilling for it. Did Masters find it difficult to maintain his detachment?

'You say that the book's not judgemental, but there's one point where I *do* come off the fence and say that the way Nilsen disposed of the bodies was disgusting. I remember telling him this. "Look, Des," I said. "I can understand that one can kill people; of course we could all do it. I can even understand how if you find you enjoy it because of some ghastly quirk in your nature you may as well do it twice or three times as once. What I cannot understand is how you could live with the remains of people in your flat, how you could actually put a head into a pot and then turn it down to simmer while you took the dog for a walk and then returned and made a slice of toast. That's the gulf that exists between you and me. I could never understand that. I never will."

' "Well, there's something wrong with you then," he said, "if you're more horrified by what I did to corpses than what I did to living people. *Your* morals are in question. The wicked thing I did was to squeeze the life out of people and that is unforgivable. But you can't hurt a corpse. It was simply something I had to get rid of and you shouldn't be horrified by that."

'But I am still horrified. I think I'm right and he's wrong. Yet the psychiatrists agree with him. In the Postscript Anthony Storr says, "Masters goes over the top a bit when he's appalled by the way in which the murderer disposed of his victims . . . " '

Does Masters consider that the public's viewing of murder as a nicely macabre diversion has encouraged murderers to become in some way conscious that to gain attention their killings have to be yet more spectacular?

'No. I've never believed that and still less do I believe it now. It seems to be perfectly incomprehensible that anyone to achieve fame would go through the trauma of actually killing someone. What makes Nilsen spectacular is the fact that he's an articulate and intelligent man and that he has such a curious psychological past that it's worth examining him. If the death penalty existed right now I would campaign like mad to stop him being hanged – not because I feel sorry for him, but because if you destroy him you destroy the only evidence you've got. What they should do is spend the next ten years examining him. Of course they don't think like that; they just let him rot in prison.'

Was there any point during the writing of the book that Masters felt a sense of revulsion towards his subject?

'At one point, yes. I had come to know Nilsen very well and I asked Scotland Yard if they wouldn't mind showing me the photographs they took, immediately after his arrest, of the human remains at Cranley Gardens. I said this was not ghoulish on my part but because I'd got to remind myself of what this man had done; I was in danger of forgetting as I was getting on so well with him. I saw the pictures; there were boxes full of them. I don't know how many . . . it must have been between fifty and a hundred. I managed to look at about twelve and then I couldn't bear any more. At that moment I was revolted. But it didn't deter me from continuing with the book. I'd got to find out why such iniquity was possible. I never felt squeamish to that degree. But I was revolted by what I'd seen and told him I'd found the pictures absolutely horrifying. "Yes. You would," he said. "Yes. You would. At times I find it quite frightening." Even he! Which may be contrived, but I don't think so. I think he's very honest with me.'

Does Masters in any way consider that today's more casual approach to sex and sexuality might have contributed in Nilsen's case to his apparent disregard for human life?

'No, it's the opposite that occurs to me. Being Scottish, Nilsen inherited a tremendously big guilt feeling in capital letters about his homosexuality. He came to London when the 1967 Sexual Offences Act was only five years old, when it was still difficult to move around the homosexual world in a way other than furtively. On the contrary, now that the whole attitude is more casual the kind of obsessive secretiveness from which Nilsen suffered is much less likely to occur and therefore is much less likely to lead to his fantasies and his murders. I think it's safer now, not less safe.

'I think the casualness is a help because it makes people healthier mentally and Nilsen was mentally extremely unstable, largely, though not exclusively, as a result of his guilt about his homosexuality. If that hadn't occurred there would have been one less influence working against him.'

Robin Maugham

Born in 1916 into a resolutely upper middle-class family (his father became Lord Chancellor in the Neville Chamberlain government: his uncle, Somerset Maugham, was one of the most successful novelists and playwrights of his day), Robin Maugham has achieved success as a novelist, travel-writer, biographer (notably of his uncle) and autobiographer.

The Servant (1948) remains his most well-known novel – though his widely regarded books also include *Somerset and All the Maughams* (1966), *The Wrong People* (1970) (a novel about homosexual obession which was inappropriately marketed as a thriller) and *Escape From the Shadows*, an explicit and honest autobiography.

There's probably no other novelist writing in England who's written for so long a period and so consistently about sexuality and the sexual motivation of character – heterosexual and homosexual. For example his first novel, *The Servant* – now I'm sure everyone always asks this, but how did he come to write it?

'Yes, I'm often asked that. And the answer is that two disparate incidents that occurred in real life somehow fused in my mind. The first incident was after the war when I'd been invalided home; I found that our country house had been requisitioned and my parents had taken a little cottage in the country where Michael Kremer, the neurologist, thought it would be a good thing for me to rest. I went and lived down there alone because my parents lived in London throughout all the bombing very happily. There I was in this little cottage. One day I was walking across the golf links when cantering by came a girl on a horse. Perhaps it was the contrast because the horse was very black and the girl was very blonde – perhaps that was what made me look at her. But in a curious way I fell in love with her. I thought she was about seventeen, and after that, every afternoon I would walk across the golf links hoping she'd ride by again. I don't know what I thought I was going to do if she did; I thought I'd wave or something. But she never came by – rode by again.

'Then one day I was going into Lewes to do some shopping and I was standing at the bus stop and there was a very young girl standing beside me. When I turned to look at her carefully, I saw it was the girl on the horse. We made friends then and there; on the bus we sat next to each other and I asked her age and she was just sixteen. I thought – I was by that time about twenty-five – I thought she's far too young for me to have sex with. She was obviously from a very respectable middle-class family. But I was still so attracted by her that I asked her to tea at the cottage and then we gradually managed to go for walks together. One very hot summer evening we were walking through a wood when we came to a clearing. She said, "Let's sit down." We sat down on a bank of turf. She said, "It was here that it happened." I said, "What happened?" She said, "You know that I was in show-jumping and I had a riding-master. One day we came to this glen and he said, the horses are sweating; let them have a rest. So we tied their reins up to a tree. We lay down on this bank and he began stroking me. He was a man of about forty and part of me was frightened, but part of me wanted him to go on. It was on this bank when we were lying there that he did it. He was very gentle, but all the same it hurt terribly. The next time, the next evening, it wasn't so bad. Then I got to love it and we'd go out every evening. I thought my mother might be getting suspicious so we made it every once or twice a week. And then I was afraid I was going to have a child. So I got into a panic and went and told Mother. Well, of course she had hysterics – she was terribly upset. She took me to the doctor and they did tests and I was all right – I wasn't going to have a child. There was nothing she could do about the riding-master without

110

me going into the witness-box to say that he'd had me. So she gave him a warning and he left the district." The girl stopped, lay back on the bank, looked up at me and said, "So you see, you needn't worry." She began to undo her dress – and that's how it all began with her. She was my mistress for over a year. Then she fell in love – she went off with someone else and I think she's now happily married.

'When the war ended my mother bought me a little house in Chelsea. I'd been abroad and when I came back she'd installed this manservant and he looked after the house beautifully, cooked terribly well and kept everything very clean. But somehow he gave me the shudders. Something about him frightened me. It seemed too ridiculous to dismiss the perfect manservant merely because he worried me by his presence. One evening I'd been out with Mary Churchill to dinner and then afterwards the cinema. I asked her back for a drink. We came up to my living room and she said she'd love a lager. I said, "I know there's two bottles in the fridge." I walked down the stairs which led to the dining room, then down the other flight of stairs which led to the kitchen and the servant's bedroom. There was no sign of Barrett but the door to his bedroom was open and, lying naked, face downwards, spread-eagled on the bed was one of the most beautiful boys of about fourteen I've ever seen. His hair was fair and curly; his skin was immaculate and his figure was lovely – his body was lovely. While I was staring in wonderment at this beautiful creature a voice behind me said, "Good evening sah, I see that you are admiring my nephew. Perhaps you would like him to come up later and say goodnight to you?" At that moment I saw the portals of blackmail and the gates of prison yawning open before my gaze. Yawning open as they met my gaze. I pretended I hadn't heard what he said – I quickly turned round – I collected the two bottles from the fridge and went upstairs; "Goodnight Barrett," I said and walked on up. When I got into the living room, Mary Churchill stared at me and said, "Whatever happened to you? You look white as a ghost." I said, "Yes; I've just seen one." But I never told her the story.

'A few weeks later when I was down in the country, I was telephoned by the police who told me that Barrett had been caught trying to pawn all my clothes. I was asked if I wanted to bring an action and I said no, I just wanted him out of the house and never to see him again. And I never have. Then a year later these two completely disparate incidents fused in my mind and I began writing – but I can't remember the actual act of writing it. I only know that I went on writing until I was so tired each day that I couldn't write any longer and I'd just fall into bed. Finally there it was – *The Servant*. It seems odd to me now, when I re-read it, how it ever happened.'

Do you think you would have written differently had you not been homosexual?

'I think it's awfully hard to say. After all, three of my books which have had the greatest successes have not been homosexual at all; because I am bisexual, though predominantly homosexual, I hope I can understand both sides, as it were. If you take *The Barrier*, *The Green Shade*, and *The Rough and the Smooth*, there are three novels in which not one queer character appears. Yet they all had successes.

'I have allowed myself more licence, I think, than more remote novelists who are kind of closet queens. After all, I got on the BBC and told eight million people that I loved boys: well, you can't be more honest than that! And I don't care.

'I think the most rewarding thing I've done is my autobiography. I've kept a file of the letters I've received from people who've read it, and they are so moving; they come from every rank, every class, every type. Some were written on crested paper. They say things like: "Having read your book, I know I can trust you not to reveal my name. But if I had *not* read your book, I would have committed suicide within the week. The fact of what you say in your autobiography has given me the courage to go on." Now that is something.

'One of the things about coming out is that quite often people say, "Why do you need to say you're homosexual?"

But, of course, the thing is, it's not so much for our own sake or for the members of heterosexual society.

'Somebody said to me, when I addressed a recent *Yorkshire Post* literary lunch, "Don't think about the people in the big towns; they'll always be able to make an arrangement. Think of somebody in a small town or a village who is a homosexual. What can he do in the present state of society? And I think that is a terrible and awful thought and *that* is why I carry on. I hammer on and I go on BBC and whenever I do, I never miss an opportunity of saying I'm queer and that I think it's absolutely splendid. I get furious with the Church and, indeed, with the State, when they say: "Do you realise that this is an abominable crime?"

'The most wonderful thing was the homosexual debate in the House of Lords. There was a great moment when some tremendous anti-queer got up to speak, and everybody made a rush for the tea bar. But not before two very old peers who knew their stuff far better than we did. They had looked at their list and seen that this old bore was going to speak and they'd got the lovely prize position in the embrasure, very good seats overlooking the river. They really ordered themselves all the teas their nannies had never allowed them. They had muffins and crumpets and honey and they were absolutely gorging themselves. Now both of them were over eighty and deaf. One said to the other: "I say, Blenkinsop, I never knew you were a bugger." Rather like a kind of prehistoric animal, it took a long time for the remark to sink in. And Blenkinsop said, "Well, I'm not as a matter of fact; I'm happily married and I've produced eight nippers." So the other one said, "You voted for them didn't you?" "To tell you the truth, I did vote for the buggers," said Blenkinsop, "and I'll tell you why. When I was a nipper myself I once had it whopped up me at school and I rather enjoyed it." Two absolutely wonderful old gentlemen.

'Then there was the one who came up to me in the corridor and said, "You know, the truth of the whole matter is, it's just a knack, like learning to ride a bicycle. Once you learn the knack, you never forget it." '

What is your reaction when people describe you as a 'gay novelist'?

'What is a "queer" novel? Is *The Second Window*, just because ten per cent of it is concerned with homosexuality? Is *The Link* homosexual? I don't regard queerness as either the normal or the abnormal, and I'm more and more convinced that, if anything, the normal is bisexuality. For instance, I have discovered most Africans, most Polynesians and most Sudanese to be pretty bisexual and we all know that we have a certain amount of both male and female chromosomes in us. I'm firmly against what might possibly be called "coterie homosexuality." It is bad, stultifying. I think it's wrong. I really do. And I think that we simply must learn how stupid it all is.

'It is very cramping for artistic impulses and it is very annoying when people ask, "Is your book queer or not?" If you've got to divide things up in, for example, *The Second Window*, eighty per cent of the characters are heterosexual. Exactly the same principle applies with *The Link*. Is it necessary to divide the characters up?

'I had the most terrible trouble over *The Wrong People* because I wrote it when I was in Ischia in a villa that I'd leased from the Waltons, the composer and his wife, whom I came to adore and still do. In the villa next to mine was Terry Rattigan. I decided that I would write this book whatever happened. So I wrote it and it was typed out and I then showed it to my uncle. Willie said, "I must tell you that I began reading your book last night in bed and I simply couldn't put it down. It's easily the best work you've ever done and I think it's perfectly excellent." Then he paused and looked at me and said, "Having told you that, I must tell you that if you publish it, it will kill you as a writer stone dead." I shall never forget my horror at those words. He said, "The public will be disgusted by it and you'll be panned by all the critics and you'll lose such little public as you've got." Then he added, "Don't be cross with me; it doesn't prevent the fact that it's an excellent book and I daresay one day – not in my lifetime, not in your lifetime – it will be published. But the interesting thing is, I don't know whether you realise it, what you've proved in the novel is that homosexuality simply doesn't work."

'I'm not sure that the book does prove that. It certainly wasn't my intention. In writing it, my intention was a very altruistic one – I wanted to expose the vile and horrible conditions that obtained in our approved schools, where young kids of twelve onwards are sent if they're in need of care and protection. And where, in one particular school, the housemaster was a vicious sadist. Now the rate of pay for masters who teach in approved schools on the Burnham scale is higher than the normal scale because of the risks involved with these tough kids. But a housemaster, as one headmaster of an approved school told me, need only have a vaccination certificate. That's all he needs – he need have no education, nothing. Well, obviously the job attracts every really vicious pervert there is. In this particular school, this housemaster would make the kids come in who had done something wrong and say, "Now look, it's either a whipping or you can let down your trousers." And then he would rape them – and hurt them most terribly. Now, I was told this by one boy from this school; and from a completely different town in England from another boy who had been at the school, I heard exactly the same story. All parts in *The Wrong People* of life in an approved school are factual. The whole thing about the master who flicked their bottoms after showers is factual, and he was the one who would rape them – he'd choose his victims and he had one dormitory which contained just boys that he'd raped. He would go in there of an evening and he'd choose the one he wanted for the night.

'But that had been my motive for writing the book; and in fact it did have an effect. People did get hot under the collar – the politicians. An enquiry was made. But as far as the homosexual side of it was concerned, I was determined to publish the book somehow, so I published it in paperback in the United States under the pseudonym of David Griffin – for some unknown reason.

'My uncle was right in as much as it didn't have much of a success in paper under the name David Griffin. But meanwhile I showed the typescript to various friends including Noel Coward, who took a violent dislike to it and said, "What irritates me about all these queer books is that they go on as if all queers were miserable, whereas as you know perfectly well you have only to look at me to see, my dear boy, that there are queers who are very happy indeed – morning, noon and night!" Well, various people took various views about it, but Terry Rattigan, reading it again, said, "Publish and be damned," quoting the Duke.

'I just write the thing for better or worse exactly as I see it coming in my mind. I hope I am writing about contemporary life as I see it and admittedly there are some absolutely queer or absolutely heterosexual people, but I'm not interested in people because they're one thing or another, or a mixture; I'm interested in them as people.'

Your writing suggests an enormous emotional vulnerability.

'Yes. You see, at the end of the war, I was still bisexual, almost I would say evenly. And you're supposed to love a girl or a boy – and I very nearly married. I'm glad now that I didn't. Not for my sake so much as the girl I almost married. Because I've seen so many marriages which go all right at first, but there comes a time when he can't take his eyes off the young waiter who's serving them at a restaurant; when his eyes wander towards the young man leaning against the bar . . . when he longs for the form of love that he once knew. He eventually becomes unfaithful to his wife. As they grow older, he's no longer attracted to the woman physically, but he's still capable of love with a young man and, indeed, enjoys it all the more because it's now his only outlet. The woman generally is sensitive and has sufficient instinct to understand all this far more than she allows it to appear that she does, which makes for a terrible unhappiness for the woman. And for a kind of guilt feeling in the man, which makes him rather cruel to his boyfriends in consequence. It's a terribly difficult problem, because if the woman can keep sex out of it after a while and is contented to be a companion, then it works. I've known that also happen. In fact, one can only generalise very vaguely in these matters, but be specific in one's generalities.'

There seems to have been a very large part of autobiography throughout your fiction. And in a kind of way it's built up to your unleashing the homosexual side of your nature in your writing. An unburdening which started in, obviously, *Behind the Mirror*, a book of yours which is constantly referred to when people are writing about the late fifties or mid-fifties homosexual novels – or homosexual novels in quotes, in fact. Culminating with *The Second Window* which has always seemed to me the dry run for your autobiography.

'Yes, I think it was. There were a lot of stories in – material in – *The Second Window* which aren't completely fiction.'

It also seems, in that book particularly, that you're working yourself out.

'Yes; but I think most of my novels have been a working of myself out from *Come to Dust* onwards. I mean, a travel book called *Nomad* was very much a working out. After all, there's nothing unique about a novelist working himself out in his novels. Willie's greatest novel is without doubt *Of Human Bondage*, which is practically entirely autobiographical.'

You suffer, and have suffered throughout your life, from remarkable ill-health. What are your views on illness and dying and death?

'To take them in order: illness, I think, in my case had a distinct effect on my writing. You see, for a start I had shrapnel in my head, diabetes, neuritis, all kinds of troubles. I have been a long part of my life – a considerable part of my life – in various hospitals. Now there I've been able to read; I've been able to contemplate, and I've been able of course in military hospitals and some civilian hospitals where I've been in public wards to observe the effects of illness on other people. The way in which men faced pain and the certain prospect of death – in an odd kind of way, I daresay that the illnesses that I have endured throughout my life since the war have been to me as a writer what Willie's stammer was to him. I have

117

been many times confined, too limited you may say, but at the same time perhaps it's given me some understanding that I wouldn't have had otherwise. So I don't regret it; in fact, when I think that but for the shrapnel coming from the air into my head during the Battle of Knightsbridge in the Western Desert I might be a lawyer – perhaps a failure by now, or perhaps a judge – when I think of that, I do realise how lucky I am. And I have no regrets at all.

'One must not be afraid of enjoying oneself in life provided that one can afford to physically, mentally or spiritually. I'm all for having a good time whenever it's possible. Dreary things have to be done for the cause of conscience which have to be obeyed, but on the whole I have learned that the important thing in life is to enjoy myself thoroughly when I'm writing. I think that I find at such moments a happiness and peace which I don't find at any other time.

'Dying or death: well, dying – I am absolutely scared stiff of any sort of pain; even the prospect of going to my extremely cautious and careful dentist fills me with apprehension. But I have been lucky in as much as for some reason which I simply cannot explain, I am not afraid of death itself.

'Let them bury me in the churchyard at Hatfield where my parents are buried, and just hope for the best. Maybe it's like walking through a door, as some people have said, or maybe one is reborn as the Buddhists believe, or maybe perhaps – this I doubt in my case – one reaches some form of nirvana and the spirit is joined in the Infinite of Godhead – or the Stuff of Godhead. I'm not sure, but I sympathise enormously with people who do most fervently believe, and I think they're lucky, they're fortunate, to be able to. So far as I'm concerned, I hope I don't die too soon – because, after all, there are so many more books I want to write.'

David Rees

Although he has written a whole shelf-full of books – winning prestigious prizes for two of his novels for children – David Rees is best known for his 1982 book, *The Milkman's on His Way*, sales of which are now well in excess of twenty thousand. 'I don't know why the book is so successful,' Rees muses, though he admits he is aware that the controversy surrounding it during the passage of Clause into Section 28 might have helped sales. Author of books for children, novels for teenagers (*In the Tent*, *Quintin's Man*) and adults (*The Hunger*, *Quince*, *The Colour of His Hair*), essays (*What Do Draculas Do?*) and travel (*A Better Class of Blond*), Rees announced in *Letters to Dorothy* (1990) that 'These stories, essays and poems are probably the last I shall write' – a prediction recently overturned when he published *Dog Days, White Nights*, a collection of essays, many on music – a first love – and many on travel.

A long-time resident of Exeter (though there was a relatively brief period in London), the following interview took place over an extended (four-hour) lunch in Brighton. Often picking up on points we'd previously discussed on the telephone, the conversation was wide-ranging – covering such things as musical motifs ('I'd rather go out and hear a live music performance, a concert or at the opera, than sit down and read a book') and religious themes ('I do think I probably write about religion quite frequently') in the novels.

It was inevitable that we should talk about Rees's responses to the political rumpus over *The Milkman's on His Way*. 'I was rather saddened by it. I had to spend four months of 1987 in the United States and as I left Parliament was discussing it. They were still discussing it when I got back. "Have they nothing better to do than discuss this book?" I thought. I didn't like people such as the Minister for the Arts saying I had done an immense amount to undermine the standards of family life. It didn't seem to me that the book had done anything of the sort. The boy's parents and his relationship with them is a very important ingredient in the text. No, I didn't like that at all. And I disliked turning on the television and looking at programmes like *Kilroy* on which all sorts of lies were told – such as that five-year-olds in primary schools in Haringey were being forced to read it. But I do like the fact that Margaret Thatcher is supposed to have bought a copy of it. I had a phone call from Gay's the Word to say that a government limousine with a flunky inside it had gone to the bookshop to buy a copy. And paid cash for it, which I thought was a pity because I would have liked to have kept the cheque and framed it. But I rather hope the controversy about the book has disappeared, though I suspect that the Conservative Party might revive it whenever they wish to bash "loony left" councils or gay men and lesbians for vote-getting purposes.'

Milkman was Rees's first completely gay novel – though gay themes had appeared in *Quintin's Man* and *In the Tent* and can be discerned as early on as *Storm Surge*. As he didn't fully come to terms with his homosexuality until relatively late in life does he consider the development of gay themes in his work in any way parallels his own progress?

'Yes, it certainly does. I undoubtedly started to write successfully and properly as I came to terms with being gay and came out. I came out when I was thirty-seven and had my first novel accepted for publication that year. That was *Storm Surge*. The two things are inextricably bound up together, there's no doubt about it. The fact that I now feel I haven't any more fiction to write is partly because I think my real active gay life has also come to an end. It's difficult to give good, convincing reasons as to why it should be so, but I think my gay life has been my perpetual source of copy, and it doesn't really exist any more.'

Does Rees think that in some way by writing so much about adolescence he has been vicariously enjoying a gay adolescence he missed? Or, if not, what has been the fascination of writing about teenagers?

'I suppose you're right – I was living out a kind of vicarious gay teenagehood. An experience I never had myself . . . but I think that's not the most important reason. There are other reasons for my writing about teenagers. One is that my own two children figure quite often in my books. I wrote about them when they were five, then when they were seven, and also when they were teenagers. It was something I felt I wanted to record and preserve, like taking a photograph. But perhaps even more important is that I taught in schools for many years, and then at a college of education, and then at a university, so twenty-five years of my teaching life were largely concerned with adolescents. And I think that quite a lot of the writing came out of that.

'Certainly some of the people I taught from time to time have appeared in the books. People often comment that I write an awful lot about and for teenagers, and I don't really know why that is so. They always seem to think that I'm very good at it, but again, I don't really claim any special expertise in the field.'

Does Rees think that a writer ever *really* knows what he or she is writing about?

'No, I think an awful lot is subconscious. And sometimes you pick up a book that you wrote ten years ago and find some paragraph or sentence and you say, "Oh, so that's what I really meant by that." There are so many things under the text . . .

'I'm sure people write on the whole because normal life isn't satisfactory. You know, wife, husband, mortgage, lover, normal hobbies and so on, children aren't satisfactory. I think that writing is a kind of constant conversation with the reader. I sometimes think of it as a sort of pacifier or dummy. Why that should be so I don't know. I've often thought of it, too, in the terms of the

Greek story of Philoctetes, the man who was marooned on a desert island, for reasons I've now forgotten, who had a terrible wound in his heel. He had a magic bow with which he could certainly shoot enough animals and birds to survive. And I think a writer is like that, he has this either real or imaginary wound; but he's also been given this magic bow, and I think he's like Philoctetes too in that he's isolated. We are very solitary and isolated people. It's a kind of reward and punishment, being what one is. Ultimately, I don't know why we do it.

'It is a compulsion, and it's just very rewarding. Yes, I think if I didn't write, I'd go crazy.'

There's clearly a strong autobiographical component in much of Rees's more recent fiction – *Out of the Winter Gardens*, for example, and *The Wrong Apple*, in which he tackled for the first time the subject of HIV. Did the latter novel precede or follow his discovering his own HIV status?

'Oh, succeeded it. *The Wrong Apple* was in many ways a very autobiographical account of what happened to me in the year I discovered that I did have the virus. Which goes right back to February 1985. That was an awful year. I think, looking back at *The Wrong Apple*, there are a number of things I'd like to alter. It's a very difficult subject to write about – HIV and AIDS – because the information is constantly changing, so what you write gets dated very quickly. I remember having an interesting conversation with Ed White on the subject of writing about AIDS and we both agreed at the time that it wasn't a wonderfully creative subject to write about. There's this problem – you had to have a character who had AIDS and was going to die, and the endless repeating . . . I think now that the judgement we came to was completely wrong. I think that subsequently there are all sorts of things I have written about which are to do with AIDS without killing off any of the characters. *The Wrong Apple*, for example, is also about the effect that HIV has on the other people – friends, relatives and lovers. All sorts of attitudes to it. You don't have to have people actually dying to write an effective story about AIDS.

'*The Wrong Apple* doesn't include anybody who dies, except somebody very minor, off-stage, who's only referred to in the book as actually having an illness. I don't think *The Wrong Apple* is an AIDS book. It's a book about HIV infection and the social consequences of having it. I also think it was a mistake on my part to have my HIV positive central character meeting a man who is HIV negative, and the two of them having a relationship that appears to be very good and lasts for many years after the book has finished. I don't think subsequent experience suggests to me that in real life that happens. I don't think HIV negatives really do want to have relationships with HIV positives, however wonderful the man in question may be. You are a minority within a minority. Untouchables, almost. To be left alone as a gay HIV man probably means you are going to continue to be alone. That's certainly been my experience, though I've got used to that very much and I'm not sure I want to alter it now.

'I haven't actually written an AIDS novel and I'm sure I won't, though I have subsequently written about AIDS in a whole variety of ways since publishing *The Wrong Apple* – in essays and short stories. I think there are a lot of different things that one can write – possibly the best thing I've written about it is a short story, *Life in Venice*, which appears in *Letters to Dorothy*. That's one of the few short stories I've written that I still look back on and feel pleased with. It's about a man with an attack of PCP and his recovering from it, and the attitudes which aren't totally sympathetic of his friends who are forced into coping with the situation. Yes, it's a nuisance to them. It interrupts their lives, and obviously it does interrupt people's lives.

'I think having HIV or AIDS, one does feel very isolated . . . I find it very difficult to talk about, Peter. Yet I don't find it difficult to talk about myself and my feelings in my books. I think it's very difficult to persuade people to pause and listen – you feel like the Ancient Mariner, gripping with your icy hand. People don't want to pause and listen; they want to get on to their next appointment . . .

'I've given up, on the whole, talking much about my own feelings about it. I tend now to write them from time to time in pieces for *Gay Times* . . . '

But does Rees think that an unwillingness to "pause and listen" is a specific of HIV and AIDS or more a specific of all illness?

'Yes, I think it's possibly to do with all illness, but it's possibly also specifically to do with AIDS. And it could just be specific to me and my particular situation. It could possibly have all three elements. People on the whole don't want to deal with illness – they have to give up time to something they'd much rather not get involved with.'

But surely that's because it's also a frightening signpost for *them*?

'It reminds them of their own mortality. That's why they don't really want to deal with it. This is certainly true. I find my own life very isolated in this sort of way. But I've certainly got used to it; I've certainly comes to terms with it, and I feel happy enough, though I spend great acres of time on my own. Whole days go by when the only people I talk to are on the phone. I've got used to it, but I don't like it. Yet I rather suspect that if a man walked into my life now I would find considerable difficulty in even making space, which in a sense is absurd, is a paradoxical situation, because obviously one would like it for any of the reasons that anybody would like it to happen.'

And how does Rees feel his HIV positive status has affected him as a writer?

'I think AIDS has certainly changed me as a writer. I think it is very instrumental in stopping me writing. I feel my life as a gay man is virtually finished, and I've got nothing left to write about and it's AIDS as much as anything that has done that, though AIDS itself has been interesting to write about from time to time. But I can't conceive of writing a novel on the subject at all, or anything very extensive. Only occasional pieces.

'But it's altered my life totally; there's no doubt about it. I'm sure it's changed me from thinking of myself as having a fulfilled, rewarding life as an attractive and active gay man into somebody who's got quite beyond these things.

I remember when my younger son, after I hadn't seen him for a long time, came home, took one look at me and said, "Dad, you've gone straight from youth to old age and left out the middle-aged bit," which I didn't think was a very flattering remark. We laughed about it, because he sort of changed his mind . . . yet I know what he means. I feel I've gone beyond middle age. I'm now constantly dealing with last things. Just in case . . .

'Yet I'm not ill. I haven't had any major opportunistic infection, and there doesn't seem to be any sign at the moment that I'm likely to get one tomorrow. But I'm very much conscious that life may not be too long. Each New Year's Eve, I just make a resolution to see the next New Year's Eve. I can't think beyond that.

'Certainly the writing is virtually finished. I've just dried up. In eighteen months, the only fiction I've written is three short stories – one of which was a commissioned piece. And I can't see my writing fiction ever again. But I have discovered that I do enjoy writing essays. I suppose that in a sense I've always been writing essays . . . '

Rees is one of the very, very few public or semi-public Britons to have acknowledged and been vocal about his HIV status. Does he feel – to use a useful cliché – he has a mission to write about the subject? How does he see the importance, for example, of the on-going series on HIV and AIDS that he has been writing for *Gay Times*?

'I don't feel I have a mission to write about the subject at all. If I do feel a kind of impulse to write, then it is often because of people's dishonesty. I think an awful lot of people tell lies about AIDS, and it isn't only *The Sun* that does so. I do think a lot of gay men tell lies about AIDS. One discovers that people are ill with something or they've died of something that is in fact ultimately, one knows, AIDS-related and they've told lies about it. People lie to their lovers; people get rid of their lovers. I'm struck as much by how badly many gay men behave when it comes to AIDS and HIV as to how well other gay men behave.

'We all congratulate ourselves on how well the gay community has met the AIDS crisis and so on – and indeed, it has. People have been tremendously altruistic in giving and so on. But we do tend to forget the bad behaviour, and there's been quite a lot of that. And I feel sometimes stung into writing on the subject of AIDS and HIV from that point of view.'

With further fiction unlikely -- and plays out of the question – is autobiography a possibility?

'I have completed an autobiography which will be published in 1992. Writing some of it was cathartic – the more unpleasant and tragic aspects of my life. Writing about certain things to do with childhood was a great pleasure, a great pleasure to recreate and relive and select from. But I think the teenage years were embarrassing. Maybe everybody's teenage years become embarrassing to them. The extent and problems to do with one's heart and so on all seem perhaps slightly absurd when one gets older. I felt writing about myself in my twenties and early thirties, which I did cover at some speed, was rather boring. Nothing interesting happened to me at that time.'

And was the process of writing autobiography also healing?

'Well, it may have been. Subconsciously, perhaps. There are certain things I feel I have got into perspective, and others about which I've said the last word.'

Peter Robins

Peter Robins, whose published work includes short story collections (*Undo Your Raincoats and Laugh!*, *Our Hero Has Bad Breath*, *Summer Shorts*), novels (*Easy Stages*, *Survivors*, *Touching Harry*) and, more recently, early autobiography (*Visits*), has been compared to Hermann Hesse (*Gay Times*), Somerset Maugham and Terence Rattigan (*The Body Politic*.) But this one-time political journalist for the BBC turned publisher (Third House was the brain-child of Robins and David Rees) and expatriate (he now lives in Rotterdam) remains modest about his achievements – though concerned about the possibilities available for younger gay writers at the outset of literary careers.

How did Third House come about?

'Quite simply. David Rees was lecturing in the States. At that time, Gay Men's Press had done two anthologies of short stories and David and I thought it was time they produced another. Richard Dipple at GMP didn't think so. I then approached Tenebris Light at Brilliance Books. He was equally adamant. "We're not doing any more short stories," he said. The next possibility was David Price at The Olive Press. By this time, David was back and we jointly approached David Price and suggested we guest-edit a new anthology of fiction by gay men. His initial reaction was quite favourable. I bashed out guide-lines – ground-rules, if you like. There was nothing at all limiting for The Olive Press. We offered David final veto on the material. This seemed to be O.K. Then David Price seemed to think David and I were making a take-over. So we looked at each other and said, "Let's do it ourselves." The book was planned as a one-off. We received one hundred and twenty submissions for what turned out to be *Oranges and Lemons*. At about the same time we were experiencing some little difficulties with GMP – and considered going on as publishers. Clearly The Olive Press was not going much further and Brilliance Books were coming and going like the Cheshire Cat.

'We were not interested in just being a vanity press. We wanted to try and do something about new British talent. The question of publishing lesbian material didn't arise because presses already existed which covered that area pretty well. We also didn't want anything confrontational with GMP. We decided we wanted to concentrate initially on new British gay fiction. *Oranges and Lemons* gave voice to a large number of new writers – Joe Mills and Philip Ridley, for example, who have both gone on to produce highly regarded novels. The next venture was a collection of David Shenton's cartoons – which was aimed at a different market but which paid for itself within nine or ten months. Which is all we ask. Profits pay for new ventures – which have included another anthology (*The Freezer Counter*), a first collection of short stories by Dave Royle (*Pleasing the Punters*) and a novel by Martin Foreman (*Weekend*.)'

Clearly, as both writer *and* publisher, you think the short story important. Is a third anthology planned?

'I *do* think the short story's important. I've always thought that frown given by publishers when the short story is mentioned is silly. They do the usual quid pro quo thing of saying, "Yes, we'll publish your short stories – but give us a novel next." In an era of airport lounges, beaches and commuter trains – and also contributing, perhaps, and without being patronising, is the probability that television has withered the attention span – there is probably more of a demand for short stories. Sales figures justify our doing a reprint of *Oranges and Lemons*, taking the print-run to five thousand – not bad for a small press, for that's all we are. No, the short story is a very viable form . . . There are no other outlets for gay short stories and this brings the danger that the supply will dry up – but it won't if Third House has a reputation for publishing them. I'm happy

– and I'm sure David is too – to provide a showcase. The standard of contributions for *The Freezer Counter* was higher than those for *Oranges and Lemons* – but when we did that first book, we didn't have a reputation. We intended to ᴅᴏ an anthology of European fiction – based on the Association of Lesbian and Gay Writers in Europe conference. We had no idea what would come in and – ultimately – there wasn't a book there. Maybe in 1992? Though we have no plans in that direction at the moment . . . '

Why is Third House concentrating on *British* gay fiction?

'Because I'd say no one else is doing so. Where is the writer of gay fiction to go in this country? Alan Hollinghurst, Michael Carson, Gilbert Adair and Tom Wakefield move from gay to mainstream publishing with great facility. But I don't think British publishing has changed that much in that everything always seems limited to those with good agents and good contacts. I hope David and I still have the idealism that enables us to take a text at face value. Once a month, we sit down and go through all the unsolicited manuscripts. Who else is doing that?

'I don't think we'd run to do a manuscript from America for the simple reason that they've got plenty of good presses of their own already . . . '

What propelled you to Rotterdam?

'For a good number or years – since the early eighties – I'd thought I'd like to move out of the U.K. My job with the BBC entailed a lot of travel – so I viewed on the cheap. Denmark was an early choice as I had some contacts there even before the first ALGWE conference. But the prices were too high. At the same time, I was going to preparatory meetings for the 1988 conference and festival in Rotterdam and liking the city more and more, and I decided to spend the summer of 1989 there as a kind of trial marriage. During that period I wrote the play *Risks* and *Visits*, a child's-eye view of the years just leading up to World War Two. I don't regret the decision. And I never thought of going to Amsterdam – that would simply have been changing one capital city for another. I find

Rotterdam sufficiently large so that one can be anonymous and the arts world in which gay men are living sufficiently small to know quite enough people.'

Is *Visits* a non-fiction prequel to the novel *Touching Harry* – with which it seems to have a loose chronological connection?

'*Visits* is certainly autobiographical – but I don't think I should be thinking only in terms of autobiography. In *Visits* I certainly have tried *not* to embroider; I've tried to avoid the "had I known then . . . " approach. Yet it's really impossible to visualise with the eyes of an eight-year-old; so I've tried to weave together as honestly as possible what I remembered and what I heard later. I've tried to give portraits of people in a particular social and cultural world. Some things are very different now – but some things have not changed. And there are whiffs and strands of gayness and lesbianism in respectable circles in the Thames Valley. I also look at my own sexual preferences and try to see how early they set.

'My next novel (*Stony Glances*) is set in 1970; the Harold Wilson government has fallen; Edward Heath is in Number Ten, and the bright dawn of the sixties is beginning to fade a little. GLF and CHE have both got going. It's not directly autobiographical, but it does take Harry from the end of World War Two to 1970. Very few of the characters from *Touching Harry* are still around. The book's about relationships and pretence in relationships. In *Touching Harry*, he is deceiving himself and others about his sexuality, and in *Stony Glances*, though the historical period is evidently more liberal, he still practises these artifices to avoid a constant, on-going deep relationship and that is *not* autobiographical.

'I always do three drafts of a book. The first is agony, getting it down on paper. Then I begin to enjoy it as I work on the second version. The third is dovetailing, smoothing the joints – until it reads as smoothly as it's ever likely to. I wouldn't want to do more work than that – for fear of working the life out of the damned thing.

'I intend to go on to a book about Africa. This will be far more factual – more like *Visits* – but I can't repeat myself. I wouldn't want to. *After You, Cecil* will pre-date *Stony Glances* . . . '

And are there any plans to utilise all those years as a political journalist to write a corridors-of-power novel?

'I won't rule it out, but not at the moment. It's likely to surface first in two or three short stories. Rotterdam is doing me good; I don't have those journalistic pressures. I've always said that journalism would never ruin me as a writer – but you are writing in journalese. This is a time of revaluation for me . . . '

Martin Sherman

We're seated at a table in the bar of the Lyric Theatre, Hammersmith – between us glasses of apple juice, a clutter of magazines and books (my copy of Joan Peyser's too-hot-to-handle *Leonard Bernstein* which Martin Sherman admits he's "longing to read" and his own copy of Lawrence Durrell's *The Greek Islands*.) My cigarettes – it's impossible to give them up – are at the ready.

Press agent Sue Rolfe has given me a quick briefing about Sherman's new play – *A Madhouse in Goa* (with Vanessa Redgrave and Rupert Graves) – which opens at the Lyric on April 28th, but before we can start discussing it we find ourselves an adult island in a sea of noisy schoolgirls. The same thought strikes us both – it's like being caught up in an open audition for *Annie* . . .

'These are some of my cast,' Sherman jokes. He is a quiet-spoken American (born in Philadelphia) who has lived in this country for years. He's best known for his powerful and moving play *Bent* – a London and Broadway hit a decade ago – about Nazi persecution of gay men. 'It's not confirmed yet,' Sherman confides, 'but there may be a special benefit tenth anniversary performance in June – with Ian McKellen reprising Max and Michael Cashman playing Horst.'

It appears ʌo that the long-mooted film of the play (originally Fassbinder was slated to direct) may finally happen with Richard Gere (who played Max on Broadway) producing as well as starring. '*Bent* is even more pertinent now,' Sherman acknowledges. 'So assuming the film happens, it will have been worth all the traumas we've had trying to get it mounted . . .'

More recently Sherman has written plays with strong central roles for women – *Messiah* for Maureen Lipman and *When She Danced* (originally with Pauline Collins and subsequently with Sheila Gish.)

A Madhouse in Goa was first announced for production some time ago. Why has it taken so long to get on stage?

'I finished it over two and a half years ago – which is interesting because there are certain things it touches on that have been in the news a lot in the past few months. It had a producer – Robert Fox – immediately, but there were problems about how we were to do it . . .

'It's a play in two parts, with different characters in each act and when I wrote it I assumed that different sets of actors would appear in each act. We worked out that this was not very wise, so we thought about doubling actors. Vanessa Redgrave immediately wanted to do it – but if you want someone very, very good, you have to wait for her. There were also problems with Robert Allan Ackerman's – the director's – schedule. So it's taken a long time . . . but this very often happens when you wait for the people you want. However, the central ingredients were there very quickly.

'You get very nervous waiting. You think "Is the world still gonna be here? Please Vanessa, don't get hit by a truck . . . "'

With delays of this length between completing a play and it going into rehearsal isn't there a danger that you'll have become a different person and – therefore – feel tempted to make changes which chime in with your own current perceptions?

'It's always taken time to get a play produced, so almost always you are a different person and therefore you have to be careful about changing things. It can be dangerous if those changes come out of who you are *now* rather than who you were *then*. You have to force yourself back to the intellectual state you were in when you wrote the play or otherwise there is a great danger of imposing something upon it that's coming out of where you are now. It's a very odd sensation. . . '

What is *A Madhouse in Goa* about? What are the themes?

'This play is an interviewer's nightmare. . . ' Sherman laughs. 'It's most difficult to talk about or explain and not give things away. There's a great deal the audience *shouldn't* know before they see it and I'm intrigued to see how the critics handle it. And, of course, you seldom sit down to write a play with all your themes carefully worked out. It's only when you finish writing it that you discover the themes.

'The play is about deception of all kinds – personal, political, artistic, sexual – and how small deceptions are parallel to and perhaps even influenced by the much larger deceptions in the world: those on government level, for instance. . .

'Also I think the play is about the need – the necessity – to place one's personal and artistic self within a social and political context and about the ways in which some people tend to withdraw from what's most frightening about the world. . . and how a few certain other people don't.'

The play covers quite a long time-span.

'The first act is set in 1966 and the second in 1990; the first is set in Corfu, the second on Santorini.'

The Greek island setting suggests the play may be about escaping from reality into hedonism?

'One of the characters has retreated to Santorini to escape a lot of the realities of the world. But it's hard intellectually to explain why I chose to set the play where I have – except that the area provokes a lot of responses in me and thus I can be creative about it. When you begin to work on a play in production you can begin to interpret what you've written because other people are now working on it . . . Whatever I say about it intellectually, it's all after the fact.

'There are a lot of metaphors in my plays that I'm not aware of when I'm writing but which I can see when I've finished. You get into a subject very deeply and when you've got to a stage where you are able to unlock your unconscious you are able to start – but you have to have the craft to channel it. It's only when your unconscious is unlocked that the play is really written . . . But because you're working on that level,

134

there are many things you are not able to talk about clearly.'

Messiah, *When She Danced* and now *A Madhouse in Goa* seem to focus on roles for middle-aged actresses. Was this intentional?

'I haven't set out to write plays for middle-aged actresses. Women are freer in their emotional lives than men and are more open to everything around them and as a result they are fascinating for a writer. Men – basically – are very uptight and you can get very constricted just writing about men because they are very constricted – including gay men. The operative word of the two is *men*. I think – by and large (though it's a gross generalisation) – women tend to have more wisdom about life and the more centred characters in my plays are women.'

How does it feel to have Vanessa Redgrave in the play?

'I've had *two* dreams fulfilled . . . One was to have Ian McKellen play in *Bent* – and even in that case it occupied only a very small part of my mind. I don't think you can think in terms of actors when you're writing, because all you end up doing is writing some kind of cliché. It's the characters who count – and characters "take over" and then very surprising things happen . . . '

And what about Goa? Where does that figure in the play?

Sherman gives a wry grin. 'That's one of the things I can't tell you,' he says.

Colin Spencer

Colin Spencer, now in his mid-thirties, made his first impressions as a painter, and, though he hasn't bothered to exhibit, he has had a considerable success. He trained for a while at the Brighton College of Art but left because he was told he'd never become a painter unless he painted what they wanted him to, which, at that time, was in the style of Sickert. 'You know,' he says, 'blurs and shades of shit.' His first published works were short stories in *The London Magazine* and *Transatlantic Review*, and these were followed by the novels, *An Absurd Affair*, which is set in Vienna; *Anarchists in Love*, the first volume of a quartet about suburban family life and standards; *Poppy, Mandragora and the New Sex*, a brilliantly funny book in the Firbank fashion; *Asylum*, originally planned as a theatre piece but, after *The Marat/Sade*, which it resembles in style though not in plot or theme, was turned into a novel. *The Tyranny of Love* is the second volume of the quartet, and, the third volume is *Lovers at War*. His first play, *The Ballad of the False Barman*, was staged at the Hampstead Theatre Club in 1966 and his second, *Spitting Image*, was staged off-Broadway and productions of it are planned in several other countries including Germany and Australia.

Mr Spencer looks younger than his thirty-five years and has a wonderfully youthful and exuberant attitude towards life. We met at his flat, which commands a superb view over North London, and talked on the terrace where he works if the weather is fine enough. He was dressed in blue, his favourite colour, chain-smoked Disque Bleu – a brand he's used for fifteen years – and his mongrel dog Candour sat with him throughout.

When did you first start writing plays?

'In the army when I couldn't paint. The first play was all Quartet material, a big family saga, Rosie . . . '

She's the painter grandmother in the Quartet . . .

'Rosie was lovely in that play. She was a great character – I suppose she stemmed from Gully Jimson. I read *The Horse's Mouth* and adored it when I was sixteen.'

So you were writing plays before novels?

'Yes. I've always been more drawn to the theatre than to novels. After that play I went on writing under the influence of Christopher Fry and Mr. Eliot, terrible metaphysical plays in blank verse.'

But still no success?

'No. Then when I was twenty-one I wrote a short story which was published in *The London Magazine* about conditions in a geriatric hospital, immediate experience transmuted into a hysterical story.'

And how were you managing to keep alive at this time?

'I sold a few drawings and paintings and a few other short stories and I suppose a bit of tarting in Vienna helped, though I was a bad tart because I never had the nerve to charge enough and I always felt too sorry for the customer. Then I wrote the first novel which sprang out of a long short story which was an awkward length for publishing so I expanded it. And after that, with great excitement, I went back to the material I really wanted to work on, *Anarchists* and the Quartet.'

How did you come to write *The Ballad of the False Barman*?

'You remember why Shelagh Delaney wrote *A Taste of Honey?*'

She thought she could write better than Terence Rattigan . . .

'Well, I'd just read a Patrick White play, *The Ham Funeral*, because I was going to design it for the Mermaid – in the end they didn't do it – and I thought it appallingly sentimental and trite. So . . . I sat down and wrote *The Ballad* and actually it got me out of a two-year writing block I'd got after *Anarchists* when I'd felt I couldn't write at all and in those two years I just painted. It's an extraordinary mixture that play, derivative of, I think, every experiment in twentieth-century theatre.'

Were you trying to say anything particular in it?

'I think it attacks the corruption in society that the English tend always to want to dismiss. A part of the plot came straight out of a Brighton local paper.'

Barman is one of the few plays I've seen which has successfully managed the marriage of techniques which European theatre has thrown up in the last thirty years or so and the influence of Genet and Brecht are most strongly apparent. Like Brecht you used music and song. Did you especially enjoy doing this?

'Yes, I do like songs and music in my plays. I want to write more plays with songs. In fact, I've got two more plays, both unfinished, that I want to work on. But now I've been commissioned to do a musical version of *Poppy* which is great fun.' (And to illustrate this he gets up and executes a strange little dance whilst singing, in a Noel Coward voice, a lyric from this project.)

Last year you did *Spitting Image*, which seemed to arouse a good deal of violent reaction here and then you went to America with it.

'Yes, it was adapted for America and ruined.'

In what way?

'I was trying to achieve, in that play, on one level the reality of a love relationship plus the added responsibility that a child gives and, on the other, a satire on bureaucracy which was pure farce. The whole play's style had to change gear constantly and I think the audiences here found that worrying. Maybe it's technically bad, but I don't know . . . I've been told that I put too many themes in my work and that I should simplify and control my material more. I think that's balls.'

Why's that?

'I think any work of art is composed of a rich variety of themes and any one novel or play for instance ought to be able to move from laughter to tragedy. With *Spitting Image* I wanted the audience to be in tears at the end of Act One and roaring with laughter at the end of the play. I achieved this with some London audiences but in New

York the play was staged in one act and had lost all the gentleness and reality. It was just a knockabout farce for queers – utterly boring. They were frightened of the real relationship between two men, the American adapter's philosophy being, "We can't open another can of peas" . . . stupid fart!'

I hear that *Anarchist in Love* is going to be made into a film.

'Oscar Lewenstein took an option on *Anarchists* nearly two years ago but he's had difficulty in finding a suitable director. I've been working on the screenplay this summer and we hope to begin filming in the autumn, with locations in Brighton. A great place, very un-English; it has an exuberance about it, an underground sordid vulgarity. My vision is extremely unpopular with the local Council.'

I gather, too, that Columbia intend to make a film of *Spitting Image*.

'Yes, I think it could be very funny with its London setting and directed with a Truffaut touch, which is exactly what it needs.'

Film and television are very similar forms; are you interested in writing for television?

'I'm fascinated with the cinema and to a certain extent with TV, but with television one's material has to be so much narrower because of censorship and I hate any kind of imposed limits on what one can say. Nevertheless, because of being a painter the visual side is very strong, and I get especial pleasure out of linking dialogue to mental pictures. The television play, *Palm Beach Blues*, sprang from a visit to Palm Beach, Florida, I made whilst I was in the States with *Spitting Image*.'

Palm Beach Blues is a particularly strong piece; it seems to show a certain disgust with its subject . . . .

'What fascinated me was this extraordinary mixture of elderly multi-millionaires and aged matrons looking for young gigolos and overfull garbage cans and a plague of rats.'

Your new play for the stage is . . .

'*The Sphinx Mother*.'

When is this likely to be staged?

'We hope to see it produced this autumn.'

How would you describe the play?

'It's a modern Oedipus which goes on from where the classical play ends . . . I think the psychology of Jocasta committing suicide when she realises she has married her son is hopelessly wrong. In the classical plays it obviously springs from society's guilt, Jocasta representing the guilt of a small tribal unit. In the complicated structure of our society the myth says quite different things to us. I think the mother/wife role must be the most powerful we can imagine, so my play is about the battle between Jocasta and the Antigone figure to possess and keep Oedipus.'

What gave you the idea for this play?

'The strong feeling that Jocasta could not, would not, behave in a self-destructive way came to me in the Peter Brook production of the Seneca *Oedipus*, a brilliant play pretentiously directed out of all recognition.'

The Oedipus myth appears in both *Asylum* and, I think, in the Quartet – with Matthew as Oedipus, Hester as Jocasta and Sundy as Antigone. Now you've tackled the theme head on, does this mean that the Oedipal story has a particular fascination for you?

He grins mischievously. 'How observant of you to see that thread in the Quartet! What fascinates me is to see ordinary suburban families laden with these archetypal myths. Some years ago there was a murder case in Brighton where a man killed his wife. In court the evidence came out that his mother had slept with her son from the age of twelve to fifteen. It was actually this case that I was thinking of when I wrote *Asylum*. It does seem to me that all families are sexually very much entwined and quite obviously a revulsion from this leads to later psychotic trouble, so if we can understand it and not fear it, it's all part of adjustment. There's no doubt that the Oedipus disturbance is the most common. In the play I'm exploring the question of whether incest is really as black as we want to think it is; after all any sexual relationship is bloody difficult, and if Antigone is aged twenty then they've obviously had many years of happy married life. Why shouldn't it continue?'

But the play ends with a question mark . . .

'That's exactly what all art ought to do; we're here to ask the questions and not give the answers. Besides, I suspect answers as they're always too simple and they close minds rather than open them up.'

The Sophocles *Oedipus* is written as three plays; does this mean that you intend to do an O'Neill and write a complete cycle as he did with the *Oresteia*?

'Well, in order to write the first one I had to create a detailed biography involving three different families going back to the middle of the nineteenth century. On the way I found I had created other fascinating characters who were needed to ensure that the myth occurred; so I would like to write two other plays, one set immediately in the post-war era when my Oedipus character was fifteen, and the last one to be Antigone's play which would be set several years after the present one has finished. Of course our main horror about incest is the biological one of genetic malformation, and there is a seventy per cent risk that offspring will be abnormal, which is the real pathos of Antigone.'

Another theme that is almost obsessively threaded through all your work, right from Sarah Howard in *An Absurd Affair* to the Jocasta and Antigone figures in the new play, is the parent-child relationship. Nowhere in your work, not even, I feel, in the novels so far published of the Quartet, is it more strongly apparent than in the "Oedipus" play, and in everything, I think, you tend to see it as something rather destructive.

'I had two traumatic experiences in my life. The first was being a son and the second was becoming a father.' (Mr Spencer was married to a childhood friend but they are now divorced. His son, Jonathan, is now eight.) 'I don't think I agree with you that I see them as destructive, though every relationship potentially is and that's why it's frightening. Children are always being sacrificed to parents' ambition and pride, and the family unit itself has enough material for a lifetime's work.'

Though I've read the new play I've yet to read the new

141

novel, which I believe has been held up by your publishers for some time.

'They were first of all worried about its length as it's four hundred pages long. In America they adore long novels, and here what do you get? Thousands of novels a year which are trivial incidents stretched out in a tenuous way with a few shadowy characters. Fifty years ago they would all have been short stories an eighth of the present length.'

You don't sound as if you approve of contemporary novelists?

'Thin and tepid stuff most of it . . . '

Surely there must be some exceptions?

'Most of them died in the last ten years. I admire Kurt Vonnegut hugely for his satire, wit and wisdom, and I have an admiration for a particular kind of feminine perception and sensibility – you find it in Olivia Manning's Balkan trilogy – but of course Forster had this raised to a great art.'

Your titles always seem to be especially fitting to the material they cover. What relevance has *Lovers at War*?

'Well, this book is a mammoth attempt to dig out the elements of destruction in a love relationship; there are two couples in the book and four sets of parents. The parents all spring from different social strains, and there is a series of sequences set when the characters are children in the period of the war. I wanted the violence of countries to be counterpointed against the violence within us so that we have some way of coping with the violence outside us.'

Your sexual scenes frequently start out seriously but end in wildest farce. Does this mean that you find sex comic?

'Yes, very, and it gets more so. Sex is absurd and love often seems grotesque; this compulsive need we have to possess the love object utterly is both sad and hilarious but it's all very much part of the fun of life, which I enjoy enormously.'

Both the characters of Reg and Matthew in the Quartet seem to bear a rather striking resemblance to you and I almost feel that you have split yourself up with Reg as your literary self and Matthew as your painter self. How true is this?

'The American reviewers got very intrigued over this; one took me out to lunch recently and I told him I was Sundy. That confused him. Yes, of course one pours part of oneself into all the characters. I'm afraid Matthew incorporates the dark, desperate and melodramatic side whilst Reg is more extrovert. Sundy, of course, is much more of a clown, like Eddy the father, but all the characters have qualities about them which I have observed in other people . . .'

So the Quartet is very much a mixture of autobiography and fiction?

'That's true, and I must say now I have no idea where one ends and the other begins; but the whole philosophical question of reality and illusion is one that fascinates me. After all, our imagination is so much more intense than the observed reality around us, and the total subjectivity we have means that there is a quite logical argument to prove that objective reality cannot exist at all. Perhaps in thirty years' time I'll attempt to write an autobiography of my early years which will try and assess what actually happened as against what I changed and distorted, though, possibly, it will be too late then to remember.'

You seem now to be fairly firmly embedded in the theatre. Does this mean you've abandoned the novel form? And where do you envisage your career going within the next three or four years and in what special field?

'I shall of course finish the Quartet but I want to take my time over writing the last volume. The theatre seems to me an immense challenge and basically so much more exciting than the novel, but, as you know, the commercial theatre we have offers very little opportunity for original imaginative work.'

Yes, and the experimental theatre seems just as hopeless. Both seem to want totally mundane works for totally mundane audiences, and even the audiences aren't swallowing so easily any more. That leaves the cinema, which strikes me as being the one comparatively healthy art form we have at the moment . . .

'Of course I'd like to do an original film as I think one has more freedom to explore the problems and, on the whole, less censorship, and a visual dexterity; yet the cinema has always seemed to me to be ersatz theatre. I'd like to get back into the theatre the elements of primitive excitement and ritual which other people have recently attempted but only through the intellect, and that's why it has seemed so pretentious.'

With all the writing that you are involved with at the moment do you still have time to do that with which you first started out – painting and drawing?

'Alas, very little; oil painting is all so messy and it needs total involvement for months on end. Lately I've never had a period when I could lock myself up in my studio and forget about every other commitment. However, I plan to do more and I shall probably end my days like Djuna Barnes and Gully Jimson, climbing huge step-ladders and laboriously painting large canvasses which will be quite unsuitable for hanging anywhere.'

Edmund White

Even though he describes his autobiographical novel *A Boy's Own Story* as 'more realistic, popular and accessible than my other novels,' Edmund White was 'totally surprised' by the critical praise heaped upon the book when it was first published in America last year.

'It makes me suspect there are other reasons for the acclaim, in the States at least,' he admits. 'The political climate there is such at the moment that I suspect the Left – such as it is – finally decided to accept Gay Liberation as a cause and once that had come about, they had to find a "literary" novel to acclaim. As *A Boy's Own Story* is about childhood and adolescence, it is more acceptable to heterosexuals. That period in life isn't really so much about gay life as about "coming out" – and it is gay life which is more repellent to heterosexuals.'

Does White think that the interest in his work is indicative of a change in Establishment attitudes towards what are termed "gay writers"?

'I do. Of course, there are other writers in the States who emerged at the same time as me. In 1978 – when I published my second novel, *Nocturnes For the King of Naples* – Andrew Holleran's *Dancer From the Dance* and Larry Kramer's *Faggots* also appeared. That started it, because all three of those books received a lot of critical attention.

'It's interesting. There is now a second generation of gay writing which is not just about "coming out"; it's about dealings with the family, things like that. There are two novels out in the States at the moment which represent two different responses to what to do with your family – one by Andrew Holleran, who is still in the closet and who

145

spends half his time writing in New York and the other half with his parents in Florida. Holleran is a pseudonym – and when he's with his parents, he tells them he works as a waiter in New York. It's funny – because just about every waiter in New York tells his parents he's a writer. The other book is *The Family of Max Desir* by Robert Ferro – which is about a gay man who is trying to get his Italian immigrant father to accept his lover.

'Another thing is that there's not that much good fiction coming out. Some of these books sell well and "literary" fiction that sells well is attractive to the literary establishment. Gays are big readers – but until recently they've not wanted to read the more sensational gay fiction that was available. Of course, there's still a feeling that gay fiction must be minor league, that it's ghettoised and genre writing. But the truth is that American life is so complex and vast and murky that it's best perceived from a minority perspective. The best American writing since the war has been by Blacks, Jews and gays.'

How does White feel about being labelled a "gay writer"?

'If a writer's good, he's classified many different ways in his own lifetime. Gay writing – if it's good and if it survives – won't be called gay writing in fifty years. Literary fiction often emerges in some kind of controversy – how many masterpieces have emerged in an atmosphere of scandal? I think, also – with fiction – with time, it no longer has the same associations as when it was published.'

White has written four books and co-authored a fifth – his first novel, *Forgetting Elena*, was highly praised by Nabokov; his second, *Nocturnes For the King of Naples*, was applauded by Gore Vidal; *A Boy's Own Story* was acclaimed by just about everyone in America ("Edmund White has crossed *The Catcher in the Rye* with *De Profundis*, J.D Salinger with Oscar Wilde, to create an extraordinary novel," proclaimed *The New York Times Review*); *States of Desire: Travels in Gay America* received enthusiastic responses from Christopher Isherwood, William Burroughs and Fran Lebowitz; and *The Joy of Gay Sex* –

146

co-authored with Dr Charles Silverstein – has the distinction of being burned by British Customs.

Does White feel that the diversity of subjects and styles has aided his acceptance by the American literary establishment?

'Because I've written in so many styles, I feel it has worked against me rather than for me. In American publishing there is a drift towards packaging, towards an author writing the same book over and over again so that the publisher knows exactly how to market it. I feel that each book should be a new theory about the novel as well as a new novel.'

How autobiographical is *A Boy's Own Story*?

'It's creative autobiography – which may be a synonym for lying. The book follows the main outline of my own life – but I've simplified and normalised things. In real life there may have been three bookstore owners who meant a lot to me; in the book I've merged them into one. I was a great deal more self-possessed than the boy in the book, but I thought if I wrote my own story it would be freakish. By the time I was fifteen I must have slept with about five hundred men; this boy has only a handful of sexual experiences.'

Does Edmund White feel that America has changed much since he travelled across it when writing *States of Desire*?

'Yes. The main preoccupation at the moment is AIDS. It has made people pull in their horns in terms of sexual adventure. It has caused a loss of confidence in being gay; people *are* feeling guilt-struck and it brings out the remnants of self-hatred. AIDS *does* feel like divine retribution. I've had people come up to me and say, "Don't you feel rotten that you wrote *The Joy of Gay Sex*, encouraging people to have sex – and now they're dying?" There is a feeling that gay men are lepers – funeral parlours won't embalm the bodies; nurses won't treat the victims. The baths are emptying; hustler ads are shrinking in number. Eighty-five per cent of Americans now know what AIDS is. "Homosexuality" was a term invented by doctors which we were stuck with for years; now after a decade of freedom the term is being re-medicalised. Once again we're becoming a medical problem, not a cultural one.

'One of the good things to have come out of this is that it has strengthened gay institutions in the United States. In the past, police raids on bars and baths have been one of the few things which stirred up gays. Now, since they are not cruising or going to the baths, people are becoming more involved.'

White, who also teaches English at John Hopkins University, has recently been awarded a Guggenheim grant and will be spending a year in Paris. What are his writing plans?

'I'm currently working on a long obsessional novel about heterosexual sex – about which I know nothing, so it's a fantasy novel.'

And gay writing?

'Gay writers have a sense of speaking for other people. Not enough has been written yet and before even the most basic aspects of gay experience have been mapped out. I would feel it wrong to start exploring some small corner. There is still so much to be written about gay life.'

Michael Wilcox

'One of the ways I work as a writer is to write about what's going on around me at the time,' explains dramatist Michael Wilcox, whose play *Rents* is currently at the Studio Theatre at the Lyric, Hammersmith. 'I originally started writing *Rents* in 1976 when I was in Edinburgh and met a character who became the prototype for Phil in the play. He told me incredible stories and took me around Edinburgh. Each day I would write a short play – lasting between three and five minutes – based on the material gleaned the day before. We would the read the play and check it for accuracy. "Phil" enjoyed it very much – my attempting to record what he said in this way, a way of relating to this particular person. It wasn't until I had amassed a collection of thirteen of these plays that it occurred to me to write a full-length play. So *Rents* arose out of my interest in a particular person – an interest I have maintained. I still see the original "Phil" in fact.'

Michael Wilcox, who lives in Northumberland, did not become a playwright until 1974.

'I used to be a school-teacher. I did a degree in English Literature at London University and back in the early seventies I was working at a Newcastle comprehensive school where I was head of the English department. I was always interested in drama and I did quite a lot of drama work with the students at the school. Then I met Cecil Taylor, who was then working in the North-West, and decided to take the plunge and become a full-time playwright. That was in 1974 and, oddly enough, I had not written a play at that point. I decided to take the plunge and wrote my first play.'

Rents – an episodic play concerned with the relationship between a Newcastle lecturer, Richard, temporarily based in Edinburgh, and two rent boys, Phil, a drama student, and Robert, a shop assistant – did not come easily to the stage.

'The play was turned down by Gay Sweatshop and the Royal Court and just about everybody else. Then it was commissioned by the Traverse in Edinburgh – but it took two years to mount. The first production was in the spring of 1979. It was very successful – both critically and at the box office. A new and revised production was staged that same year at the Edinburgh Festival – and a commercial management then optioned the play for the West End. But though they tried on various occasions to get the play on, things transpired which halted the production – which is why it has not been staged for three years. The rights reverted to me last year, enabling me go ahead with the production at the Lyric.

'The version to be seen at the Lyric is more or less the same as that seen at the Edinburgh Festival. I've not radically rewritten it. *Rents* has to be accepted as a mid-seventies play, which was when it was written. the details of prices and incomes which the characters talk about are way out of date. But you can go on rewriting for ever. So I have only done some slight bits of rewriting; I've taken out some scenes and added others.'

After the success of *Rents* at the Traverse, Michael Wilcox became the Thames Television resident playwright at that theatre for 1980-1981. His play *Accounts* is also being recorded for BBC Radio Scotland and televised for Channel Four. A joint winner – with Hanif Kureishi – of the 1981 George Devine Award for new work, Michael Wilcox's latest play, *Cricket*, has just been televised in the *Plays for Tomorrow* series.

The characters in *Rents* – to my mind – do not have much to look forward to; does Michael Wilcox consider it a pessimistic play?

'When *Accounts* came to London last year, I was described in *The Guardian* as an optimistic playwright. Considering some of the dangers some of the characters in *Rents* get into, none of them get wiped out . . . When it comes to the really dangerous moments, they survive. It's a very *optimistic* play from that point of view. My own suspicion about what will happen to those characters is that Phil will become a fairly successful criminal of a sort and Robert could pull himself out of it – it all depends on who he meets and who is willing to take him on. That's one of the redeeming aspects of the gay scene. But you really can't tell; they have survived. However, I'm not going to write *Rents Two* or *Robert Goes to Nottingham*. Though I'm tempted to write about Spider.' (One of the characters in the play.) 'Originally, he appeared in only one scene but I wrote in a second scene by popular demand – people wanted to see more of him.'

The success of *Rents* at the Traverse engendered some strange stories – and some odd audience responses.

'The theatre was packed out night after night. People turned up time and again. One guy appeared at the box office and asked for seven tickets. "What night do you want them for?" the person in the box office asked. "I'd like one for Monday night," he said, "one for Tuesday; I can't make it on Wednesday, one for Thursday . . . " and so on. There was also the night when, just at the end of the first act, when the two boys are undressing for bed and both are naked on stage, a loud voice was heard from the audience; "Eeh, look, that one's been circumcised!" On another night, the actor who had been playing Eddie' (threatening, violent and with more than a touch of the queerbasher about him) 'was beaten up by a bunch of gays outside the theatre. They couldn't dissociate the actor from the role he was playing.'

How have gays responded to the previous production of the play?

'The response to *Rents* in the past has been very positive – which is pleasing because it might have been seen to reinforce some people's view of the gay scene as ugly. But the play is meant to be about people rather that politics or sociology. I don't really like propaganda plays or politically motivated plays – though I was quite interested in them at one time. The trouble with propagandist or political theatre is that if the writer's own politics and point of view are too obvious, then it affects what happens in the play in too obvious a manner and the audiences very quickly press their reject buttons. In a way, I feel the way *Gay News* and gays whom I've talked to who have seen the play responded showed a certain strength. *Rents* could be seen as a terrific antidote to the propagandist plays that had gone before. But the justification of any writing is: is this true? If what is written is true to character and situation then no one has the right to shoot you down. But if it does not ring true – if there is no credibility and truthfulness – *then* they can.'

And future plans? A film version of *Accounts* is projected; a new play called *Midnight Feast*, set in a not particularly famous public school, commences filming for Scottish Television in Glasgow in May; a new play for the Travers – also to be filmed by the BBC – is in hand and, most excitingly for Michael Wilcox, he has just finished the first draft of a play for one of the London commercial managements.

Kenneth Williams

Had he been born Japanese, by now Kenneth Williams would have been declared a Living National Treasure. The diminutive but dapper star of everything from Shaw's *Saint Joan* to the *Carry On* films, plays by his friend Joe Orton and a sometimes seemingly ceaseless series of appearances on television chat-shows, has managed to turn his way of life into an art-form. Possessed of an instantly recognisable voice (an emphatically camp drawl with clear-as-a-bell diction) and a pair of famously flaring nostrils, Williams has managed that most difficult of feats – certainly appearing to be as camp as Christmas, yet presenting himself in such a way as to remove all trace of sexual threat, and thereby turning himself into something of an institution, a comic who has endeared himself to millions.

A dedicated diarist, more recently Williams has published *Backdrops: Pages from a Private Diary* and *Just Williams: An Autobiography*. The latter is an extraordinary work of self-revelation – though it's no kiss-and-tell memoir. One line in the book particularly stuck in my mind: Williams's several-times-repeated assertion that the act of falling in love is an invasion of privacy. Has this belief been a rule by which he has lived?

'I suppose in the beginning of conscious thought . . . yes. But I think that before that it was a question of instinct. I think I instinctively always knew that it would render me vulnerable and I never wanted to be that.

'I suppose that would have come from school. All the early experiences of living communally are "school" fundamentally. I was never good at any games. I was never any good at anything involving physical prowess. Consequently I very quickly became aware the only way to guard against that was to be toady for the "big one". I found the biggest boy in the school and I got well in with him and I invented a game called Our Game. I always constructed plots in which he was the King and I was the Prime Minister. I would say, "You're the king and there's a coup. They're rising up, the crowd. They're all screaming, but you don't give way. You go out onto the balcony and say 'Peace,' and you put them all down and *you* have a coup and you go back and shoot the Prime Minister. You say, 'Here's where you get your just deserts.'" And he would say, "Yes, that's good. I'll say that." And he would do all these lines, you see. And he liked this. He hadn't the capacity himself, but he liked someone providing lines and it all looked as though *he* was doing it whereas *I* was really doing it.

'I think I was feeding the imaginaton, d'you see? Certainly it was a way of keeping in with strength, because if anyone threatened me, they got bashed by *him*. He'd knock their teeth in. I was frightened to death of anything to do with fisticuffs. I always stayed with the big boys and got round them and found any Achilles heel they had. Definitely at school I was aware of the awfulness of vulnerability. I suppose you could say that was the beginning of instinctive knowledge. Later on you start to rationalise your thoughts and start to develop a philosophy of your own as a conscious thinker. That's how I came to a sentence like "All love is an invasion of privacy."

'I came to value privacy enormously, if only for the thing of shutting the door and knowing you're safe. I do value it – and I wouldn't share very well with anyone. I know *that* from a thing like lending a book and bitterly regretting it. I mean, while it's away I think it should be back on the shelf where it belongs and "What are they doing with it?" and "Will it come back dog-eared?" and "Will it be treated properly?" I've even had occasions when I've asked for a book back and been told, "Don't talk so foolishly, Kenneth. You know you didn't lend it; you said I could keep it." I never said it but they'd invented it and come to believe it.

'I mean, Gordon Jackson said on the Russell Harty Show that he'd met me when we were both in Orson Welles's production of *Moby Dick*. Gordon said that Orson called a break in rehearsal at eleven o'clock. He said Kenneth Williams came up with an outstretched hand and said, "My name is Williams and I'm the only one in this cast worth knowing. Come and have a coffee with me." And he got a laugh when he said this because he did an impression. Afterwards I said that I'd never said that, that I don't go up to people and say things like I'm the only one in the cast worth knowing. Now I really don't know, in fact, whether it's truthful or untruthful. But over a period of time, the thing gets said and starts to be accepted.'

There is a curious process that anyone writing autobiography goes through; that is, they find they are shaping their life. Did Williams find this true when he was writing *Just Williams*?

'Yes. But I wouldn't have been able to attempt a life, believe me, without the diaries. I mean, I remember talking to Stanley Baxter about this business because he'd asked me if I'd ever been asked to write my life story. "Yes," I said. "So have I," he told me. "I can't face it. All that white paper; I'd go snow-blind." And he said, "Anyway, these life stories – they're as you remember and the memory plays very funny tricks." Very often that's to compensate for a sense of inferiority, or people make up a version of what occurred to flatter their own egos. But seldom does one put it all down, warts and all. I suppose I wrote the truth, because it was awfully painful to write the book and about half-way through I packed it in.

'It was like daily lowering a bucket into the ocean and it was coming up from the ocean-bed with all these bits – because the diaries are all bits. It's not the whole truth. You put down bits, don't you? And you're coming up with all these bits and some of them are not pleasant.

'There's one thing I wished so much could be un-written, expunged. I've been associated with Dr Barnardo's for charity work since I was a child, and this incident dates from about the age of fourteen, when I'd been writing as a pen-friend to a Barnardo boy who was training for the navy. We corresponded regularly and then there came a point at which the headmaster wrote to my parents to say my pen-friend was about to be taken into the navy and that it would be nice if he and I could meet when he passed through London on his way to the base. My parents agreed, but I was appalled because it had been a relationship on paper. I instinctively knew it wouldn't work. There was this big fellow in the house whom I didn't really know how to talk with. On paper you select things to say, but in conversation it's got to be immediate and either you feel an immediacy and a natural, involuntary desire to converse or you don't. We really hadn't much in common – he was a football-playing type of boy and I didn't really play football. At this time I was an apprentice draughtsman and I came back from work one day to find a belt missing. I said to my parents: "My belt's gone." They said: "Jim's taken it because he wants to wear civvies and to keep his flannels up he used that belt. But you don't mind." But I did mind. "It's my belt; nobody's got any right to touch my things," I said. I was a very sulky, arrogant creature. I thought everything should belong to me personally. I *hated* sharing. When Jimmy came back I told him to take off the belt. "You've no right to touch my things," I said. He was surprised. "I'm sorry," he said, "I thought you wouldn't mind." "How dare you!" I said, and took back the belt. I've written it all down, and when I was looking back through the diaries I found it horrible, nasty, unpardonable rudeness to somebody who very much needed affection and security. But there is no way of apologising now, because his ship was torpedoed. Looking back, I realised what an awful lot of nastiness there was, so I packed in writing the book.

'My editor asked me why I was stopping. "It's too awful," I said. "I don't like this picture of myself." He convinced me to go on with it. "Don't worry if it doesn't sound too complimentary," he said, "because that's what life's all about. People will like you for it, for admitting that you've been naughty or whatever." So in the book I write about taking the piss out of the masters at school and playing tricks. You know, I play quite a few . . . so I mention being naughty on the set of the *Carry On* films and putting people up to things - as I did when I was working with Alec Guinness in *Hotel Paradiso*. There's a lot of that in me, which is, I suppose, sheer malice.

'When Hugh Paddick and I did Jule and Sandy in *Round the Horne*, Marty Feldman wrote me that sort of character. "It's part of you," he told me. "I heard you backstage, egging people on. Telling them to go up to the producer and complain that a line's rubbish and should be cut. This is all a little intrigue you enjoy and that's how I've come to create this character. People will find this manic quality funny." And it is very much a side of my character. But I think the humour redeems the cruelty, the black humour. The man on the *Titanic* saying, "Waiter, I know I ordered ice . . . but this is ridiculous," is funny because it's ludicrous yet it enables us to laugh at things which are really intolerably sad. It's a safety valve.'

As an actor, Kenneth Williams's personality has now become so distinctive as to have become a hindrance when it comes to being offered straight acting roles. As a man, he seems destined – albeit by choice – to spend his life alone. A curiously contradictory individual – admitting to attractions to other boys when at school, essentially virginal, yet possessing a successful career built, in part, at least, on bawdy and innuendo – Williams finds pleasure in his religious faith. Outspoken and outrageous, how would he wish to be remembered?

'I'd like to be remembered for being quite funny; if I'm going to be remembered I'd like it to be for giving people a laugh . . . Because laughter takes your mind off adversity, off the pressures to which life subjects us all. Whether we like it or not, we all lead lives of quiet desperation . . . '

Biographical notes

Neil Bartlett. Born U.K., 1958. First attracted attention as a performance artist; devised and appeared in *A Vision of Love Revealed in Sleep*; translated Racine's *Bérénice* for the National Theatre. His first book *Who Was That Man?* is a meditation on Oscar Wilde. His first novel – *Ready to Catch Him Should He Fall* – appeared in 1990. Interviewed 1990.

Peter Burton. Born U.K., 1945. Features and Reviews Editor of *Gay Times* since 1982. Has contributed to a wide range of publications – including *Adam International Review*, *Books & Bookmen*, *Gay News*, *The Independent*, *The Literary Review*, *New Society*, *The Stage* and *Transatlantic Review*. Author of *Rod Stewart: An authorised biography*; *Parallel Lives*; co-author *The Boy From Beirut*; editor *The Black Tent and Other Stories*. Two plays staged, *A Bridegroom in My Death* and *Leaving It All Behind*.

Steven Corbin. Born U.S.A., 1953. His first novel *No Easy Place to Be* was published in 1989. He is currently working on a second novel, *Fragments That Remain* (extracts from which have appeared in *Gay Times*.) Interviewed 1989.

Quentin Crisp. Born U.K., 1908. A former artist's model. His autobiography *The Naked Civil Servant* was published in 1968, but recognition came only in 1974 when the book was filmed. Has since published several books and found an eccentric international celebrity as guru, performer and writer. He now lives in New York. Interviewed 1981.

Patrick Gale. Born U.K., 1962. His novels include *The*

Aerodynamics of Pork, Ease, Kansas in August, Facing the Tank and *Little Bits of Baby*. He is a regular reviewer of books for the *Daily Telegraph*. Interviewed 1989.

Damon Galgut. Born South Africa, 1963. His first novel, *A Sinless Season*, was published when he was seventeen. His second book, a collection of short stories, is *Small Circles of Being*. Interviewed 1988.

Stephen Gray. Born South Africa, 1941. Poet and novelist and champion of the work of William Plomer. Edited *The Penguin Book of South African Stories* and *The Penguin Book of South African Verse*. Novels include *Time of Our Darkness* and *Born of Man*. Interviewed 1988.

Joseph Hansen. Born U.S.A., 1923. After publishing several gay novels under various pseudonyms, he found fame with a sequence of thrillers – beginning with *Fadeout* – featuring Dave Brandstetter, a gay investigator of insurance claims. Interviewed 1987.

Patricia Highsmith. Born U.S.A., 1921. Her first novel, *Strangers on a Train*, was filmed by Alfred Hitchcock. She is the author of an impressive succession of psychological novels of suspense, notably a sequence featuring the sexually ambivalent Tom Ripley. Interviewed 1986.

Alan Hollinghurst. Born U.K., 1954. He is deputy editor of *The Times Literary Supplement*. His first novel – *The Swimming-Pool Library* – was a huge international success. Interviewed 1988.

Timothy Ireland. Born U.K., 1959. Published two novels for teenagers before achieving wide recognition with *Who Lies Inside*. His most recent book is *The Novice*. Interviewed 1989.

Christopher Isherwood. Born U.K., 1904, died U.S.A., 1986. Most famous for his two Berlin books – *Mr Norris Changes Trains* and *Goodbye to Berlin*. Though he had a long and productive career, he never quite fulfilled the promise of his early books. Interviewed 1977.

Francis King. Born Switzerland, 1923. His first three novels were published while he was still an undergraduate. A prolific writer of short stories and fiction – his major novels include *A Domestic Animal* and *Act of Darkness* – he has also written biography and travel books. He is a regular reviewer for *The Spectator*. Interviewed 1976.

Larry Kramer. Born U.S.A. Nominated for an Academy Award for his screenplay for *Women in Love*. His novel *Faggots* was highly contentious when first published, but has been treated more seriously in recent years. A highly vocal AIDS activist, his play *The Normal Heart* was staged in London in 1986. His most recent book is *Reports From the Holocaust*. Interviewed 1986.

Hanif Kureishi. Born U.K., 1954. Playwright and screen-writer – notably *My Beautiful Laundrette* and *Sammy and Rosie Get Laid*. His first novel *The Buddha of Suburbia* developed further themes from his films. Interviewed 1990.

Gavin Lambert. Born U.K., 1924. Initially a screenwriter (*Sons and Lovers* and *The Roman Spring of Mrs Stone*), his novels include two classics about Hollywood: *The Slide Area* and *Inside Daisy Clover*. A film historian, his most recent book is a biography of Norma Shearer. Interviewed 1976.

John Lehmann. Born U.K., 1907, died 1987. A distinguished and highly influential editor (*Penguin New Writing*, *The London Magazine*) and publisher, he was a poet, biographer (Rupert Brooke, Edith Sitwell, Virginia Woolf) and novelist (*In the Purely Pagan Sense*.) Interviewed 1976.

Brian Masters. Born U.K., 1939. He is author of *The Dukes*, *Dreams About H.M. The Queen*, *Now Barabbas Was a Rotter*, (a biography of Marie Corelli) and *Killing For Company* (a study of the mass-murderer Denis Nilsen).

He is currently working on a biography of E.F. Benson. Interviewed 1985.

Robin Maugham. Born U.K., 1916, died 1981. Nephew of W. Somerset Maugham, from whose shadow he never really escaped. Best known as a novelist – including *The Servant*, *The Second Window* and *The Wrong People* – he wrote two books about his famous uncle (*Somerset and All the Maughams* and *Conversations With Willie*), two volumes of autobiography, travel books and plays. Interviewed 1976.

David Rees. Born U.K., 1936. A prolific writer of books for children (*Storm Surge*, *Quintin's Man*, *The Exeter Blitz*) and more latterly novels such as *The Milkman's On His Way*, *The Hunger* and *Out of the Winter Gardens*. He has also published the autobiographical *A Better Class of Blond* and volumes of essays. Interviewed 1991.

Peter Robins. Born U.K., 1932. Author of several collections of short stories – *Undo Your Raincoats and Laugh!*, *Our Hero Has Bad Breath*, *Summer Shorts* – novels – *Easy Stages*, *Survivors*, *Touching Harry* – and autobiography – *Visits*. Now lives in Rotterdam. Interviewed 1991.

Martin Sherman. Born U.S.A. A playwright whose work includes *Messiah*, *When She Danced* (about Isadora Duncan), *A Madhouse in Goa* and *Bent* (about the Nazi persecution of homosexuals.) Interviewed 1989.

Colin Spencer. Born U.K., 1933. A painter and novelist (*Anarchists in Love*, *The Tyranny of Love*, *Lovers at War*, *The Victims of Love*, *Poppy, Mandragora and the New Sex*), dramatist (*The Ballad of the False Barman*, *Spitting Image*, *The Trial of St George*), and, more recently, a prolific writer on vegetarian food (twelve books and a regular *Guardian* column.) His most recent book is the autobiographical *Which of Us Two?* Interviewed 1970.

Edmund White. Born U.S.A., 1950. Novels include *A Boy's Own Story* and *The Beautiful Room is Empty*. He is the author of *States of Desire: Travels in Gay America* and co-author of *The Joy of Gay Sex*. His most recent book is a biography of Genet. Interviewed 1983.

Michael Wilcox. Born U.K., 1943. A dramatist whose work includes *Accounts*, *Rents*, *Lent* and *Massage*. He has edited four volumes of *Gay Plays* and contributes to *Opera Now*. His most recent work is an autobiographical book called *Outlaw in the Hills*. Interviewed 1982.

Kenneth Williams. Born U.K., 1926, died 1988. Actor, highly idiosyncratic comedian and raconteur, his books include *Backdrops* and *Just Williams*. Interviewed 1985.

Index